Readings in Literary Criticism 17

CRITICS ON ROBERT LOWELL

Readings in Literary Criticism

CRITICS ON
ROBERT LOWELL

Readings in Literary Criticism
Edited by Jonathan Price

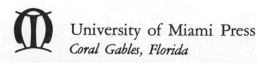

University of Miami Press
Coral Gables, Florida

Copyright © 1972 by University of Miami Press
Library of Congress Catalog Card No. 78-161435
ISBN 0-87024-210-5

Since this page cannot legibly accommodate all of the copyright notices, the pages following constitute an extension of the copyright page.

Manufactured in the United States of America

For Robert Osgood, who taught us that grammar could be our friend.

CONTENTS

ACKNOWLEDGMENTS

Robert Brustein: from *The Old Glory*. Copyright 1965 by Robert Brustein. Reprinted by permission of the author.

C. Chadwick: from *Essays in Criticism*, vol. 13, 1963. Reprinted by permission of *Essays in Criticism*.

Irvin Ehrenpreis: from *American Poetry*. Copyright 1965 by St. Martin's Press, Incorporated. Reprinted by permission of the publisher.

Geoffrey Hill: from *Essays in Criticism*, vol. 13, 1963. Reprinted by permission of *Essays in Criticism*.

John Hollander: from *Poetry*, vol. 95, 1959. Copyright © 1959 by The Modern Poetry Association. Reprinted by the permission of *Poetry*.

Randall Jarrell: from *Poetry and the Age*. Copyright 1955 by Random House, Inc. Reprinted by permission of the publisher.

Louis Martz: from *The Yale Review*, vol. 59, 1969. Copyright © 1969 by Yale University. Reprinted by permission of *The Yale Review*.

Jerome Mazzaro: from *The Poetic Themes of Robert Lowell*. Copyright © 1965 by The University of Michigan Press. Reprinted by permission of the publisher.

William Meredith: from *The New York Times Book Review*, June 15, 1969. Copyright © 1969 by The New York Times Company. Reprinted by permission.

Richard Poirier: from *Book Week*, Oct. 11, 1964. Copyright © 1964 by the *Chicago Sun-Times*. Reprinted by permission of the publisher.

Jonathan Price: from *Works*, vol. 1, 1967. Copyright © 1967 by AMS Press, Inc. Reprinted by permission of the publisher.

Christopher Ricks: from *The New Statesman*, Mar. 26, 1965. Reprinted by permission of *The New Statesman*.

M. L. Rosenthal: from *The Nation*, Sept. 19, 1959. Copyright 1959 by *The Nation*. Reprinted by permission of the publisher.

John Simon: from *Book Week*, Feb. 20, 1966. Copyright © 1966 by the *Chicago Sun-Times*. Reprinted by permission of the publisher.

Desales Standerwick: from *Renascence*, vol. 13, 1960. Reprinted by permission of *Renascence*.

Hugh B. Staples: from *Robert Lowell: The First Twenty Years*. Copyright © 1962 by Farrar, Straus & Giroux. Reprinted by permission of the publisher.

Allen Tate: from *Land of Unlikeness*. Reprinted by permission of the author.

William Carlos Williams: from *The New York Times Book Review*, April 22, 1951. Copyright © 1951 by The New York Times Company. Reprinted by permission.

INTRODUCTION:
CRITICISM MAY HELP US DESPITE ITSELF

Criticism may help us despite itself. Lowell's poetry, despite its apparent artlessness, is in one sense a form of criticism, writing about life and writing, as all art must. But in general, a good critic feels he is solving a problem when in fact he is most useful to us merely for having pointed out the existence of the problem itself. And with Lowell, though we may disagree with individual arguments about him and particular analyses of his poems, I hope we can find, in a book like this, a fairly wide sampling of opinion and a good sense of the major things which have struck intelligent and sympathetic readers as important, artistically exciting, or unsettling in his work. For Lowell himself has never been without good critics. Allen Tate wrote an introduction to his first volume that is still startling to us, in its concision and force. Tate, of course, had been advisor, confessor, and friend to Lowell for several years before this volume (*Land of Unlikeness*, 1944), and it was through Tate that Lowell came to know John Crowe Ransom and Randall Jarrell at Kenyon. It is little wonder then that "I was also reading Hart Crane, and Thomas and Tate and Empson's *Seven Types of Ambiguity;* and each poem was more difficult than the one before, and had more ambiguities." (Lowell in 1961). When Lowell went to L.S.U. (1942-3), he met Cleanth Brooks and Robert Penn Warren, who were editing *The Southern Review,* and they too offered that best kind of approval, which encourages a man's talents. Lowell's talents were certainly in the kind of metaphysical verse sought out by each of these men in his own way; and Lowell's conversion to Catholicism and his outrage at the bombing in World War II gave him two themes that could keep his passions working at a fierce heat, even in the most entangled complexities of his verse. Randall Jarrell's review of *Lord Weary's Castle* illustrates the exhilaration these men felt when Lowell's work first appeared. Jarrell stressed the violence of the conflict within the verse, the strain of opposites, nearly out of control, something Tate had remarked on a few years before; but Jarrell pointed out how often Lowell's poems take on a distinct pattern, a movement "from what is closed to what is open," a movement I would discover in his career as a whole, a gradual self-liberation and expansion. Jarrell felt this movement was tied up with Lowell's rebellion against the old New England, the Boston he had grown up in, Calvinism—much that restricts and chokes a man. And Lowell, like any rebel, still felt so bound to an obscure tradition of intense discipline—one which the Puritans had long since abandoned, and one that he could now only find in Catholicism—and a rigor of verse known only to a few of his contemporaries, that he made each of his poems into a sharp instrument. There is no slack there. As Jarrell says, he has been tough enough to tame his own rhetoric,

to make it talk for him. Again, Jarrell points to Lowell's habit of choosing
grotesque and yet appropriate "particulars" for each of his poems, and argues
that in leaving such unassimilated hunks alone, he attains a kind of drama: "He
does not present themes or generalizations, but a world—and the differences
and similarities between it and the ordinary one bring home to us themes,
generalizations, and the poet himself."

What Jarrell liked, other men disliked. Will C. Jumper,* for instance,
accepted much of what Jarrell said, but he turned it against Lowell, as a kind
of accusation. Where Jarrell was struck by Lowell's Catholicism and radicalism,
Jumper disapproved of both. Where Jarrell praised Lowell's blend of traditional
forms with his own violent feeling (what Jarrell called "the degree of intensity
of his poems" equalled their degree of organization), Jumper found the organization psychotic and the forms in disarray. Worst of all, for Jumper, was "the
extremely private nature of the concepts." But it is interesting that Jarrell and
Jumper hit on the same problems over and over again. What is important is
not how one man explicates these, or declares them inexplicable. What is
important is that each of us, reading the poems, finds himself struck most by
just these aspects of the verse.

In a good poet, we are meant to be struck by these things. And for all that
critics disagree on everything else, they do, often, tend to home in on a series
of central arguments. Their debate reveals what aspects of the work have struck
reasonable men as important or distinctive. That—more than their conclusions—is the real value of such controversy. The fact of violence, the fact of
almost metaphysical references, these facts, these words, not their interpretations are what Lowell wanted us to notice, that is, assuming he is a good
enough poet to make us notice what he wants. I think he is. The question then
becomes, why does he want us to notice such things? What is he doing with
the poem, and with us? The answer, and it must be stated with great care, lies
with each of us. For unlike second-rate verse, these poems mean a great deal
more than any one of us would care to admit, and our own answer is always
just that: our own.

Lowell is violently attracted to and repelled by Catholicism, Calvinism,
tradition, himself, his own feelings, his own world, and violence itself. War
and mental schizophrenia are his metaphors. What causes suffering for him,
being torn apart in this way, makes his art infinitely more valuable. Instead
of telling us about the world, he shows it to us, dipped in the strong stain of
his own personality.

We are drawn in, and depending on our own prejudices, we take Lowell to
be on our own side, for a moment, and then, in the next line, on our enemy's.
We are therefore drawn further into the verse, trying to find out for sure "just
what Lowell thinks." This activity, this hard thinking about his verse, is what
Lowell most wants; in his early works, he admits he almost consciously made
his poems as difficult as possible, for just this reason. "What better immortality
is there for poetry than this: continually to be vibrating in our minds?" he
seems to be saying.

---

*Will C. Jumper, "Whom Seek Ye?" *The Hudson Review,* 9, No. 1 (Spring 1956), 117-25.

I take most critical debates as intended, as set up in fact, by the author himself. I think Lowell meant us to worry about several things in his verse. And I would say that his choice of ambiguities is a clue to his importance. Lowell's sibylline deliberateness grew in the years after *Lord Weary's Castle*. In fact, the next major movement on which most critics would disagree with vehemence begins in *The Mills of the Kavanaughs*. Mazzaro sees a great falling off here. He is worried about Lowell's failure to achieve mystical vision. This is a major problem in Lowell. Should he attain some mystical communion with God, or not? Your answer, of course, depends on whether you believe in God or not. And whether Lowell does. By raising this central ambiguity (central to each of us, in that we build so much on this one tacit assumption), Lowell tantalizes, and unsettles each of us, particularly the men who wanted to see Lowell as purely a poet of religion, or Catholicism.

As the constrained existentialism of "Skunk Hour" begins to show itself, we find Lowell moving away from the more affected elements of his earlier style. Even William Carlos Williams can detect virtues in these poems. Williams is a poet who has had more influence on Lowell than is generally recognized, and Williams seems to have sensed it in his comments on the change in Lowell's style. For Williams, the important verse comes when Lowell "shoulders the rhyme aside."

Lowell will do that more often in the years to come. As before, this movement will distress some, and elate others; *Life Studies* brought sharp comment from both camps. For during the fifties, by something of a general consensus, Lowell began to seem important, and from envy and fear, the attacks increased, just as the enthusiastic applause began to be louder. John Hollander quite rightly points out that the continuities are stronger than the divergences, in *Life Studies;* both the style and the subject material come from Lowell's earlier verse, but with the new influence of Elizabeth Bishop appearing, Lowell does begin to loosen his forms and talk more easily. Fluidity is his attempt to find his own voice, and with the decision to deal with matters directly concerning him—his past, his relatives, his own stays under psychiatric care—Lowell has temporarily foregone the apocalyptic vision in order to look closely at his own.

This raises a question about the nature of these poems, in fact, about all poetry. Lowell's virtue and his challenge to critics is that he appears at times to have smelted together the three styles of poetry which Joyce distinguished; he gives the impression that he is giving you "an intense moment of feeling"; that he is brooding on himself as the center of an epical event; and that the characters in the poem do manage to take on their own dramatic life. He combines the closest and most passionate examination with the highest form of aesthetic distance. As Poirier has said, Lowell has discovered that persons and things are not something else, something larger, that they are what they are, and yet, at the same time, we feel that they are mere objects in his rampage. These are the things he sees, in his anguished outburst. They are what he seizes on. Lowell makes it difficult to dismiss any of his work as lyric, or epic; it is both; it is more, it is poetry. Each critic must deal with this problem in his own way. M.L. Rosenthal tries to explain how Lowell escapes the narrowness of self, in his poems about himself, and in the midst of a "confessional," how

Lowell manages to make the poetry into a greater structure, which Rosenthal finds comparable to *The Bridge* or *Mauberley*.

Each of Lowell's books is just such a carefully arranged structure; this is something that is true even in *Imitations,* as Geoffrey Hill notes. To me, the most powerful such sequence is that of *The Mills of the Kavanaughs,* but Lowell has refined the technique so that *For the Union Dead* appears to be an extremely complex fantasia on many of these same themes, including that of structure itself.

Imitations raises another major problem, that of how Lowell reworks earlier poets. Lowell's imitation of earlier authors is a more complex and a more original process than that of many poets since the Romans themselves. Lowell is not just copying similes, nor is he aping a manner; like Vergil, he is borrowing what he needs, freely, with full expectation that we will recognize the borrowing, and that our recognition will add to our pleasure as we see how he has changed the emphasis and re-cast the style, turning the whole to his own purposes. As Geoffrey Hill implies, what is most important is the play between the original and the "imitation."

An almost Roman sense of the classics, and a classical fondness for such imitation—these enrage, or over-awe, depending on one's nature, but, as Hill says, whatever our opinion, we would agree that Lowell "exacerbates the original." (C. Chadwick is included for his complaints about such matters, and for his attack on Lowell's distinction between meaning and tone when Lowell attempted to explain what he was doing in *Imitations.*)

In just this way, Lowell's verse seems difficult and stand-offish to many men brought up on Yeats and Eliot. As Richard Poirier says, his verse seems aristocratic, and at times it is so prickly that one cannot find entry; in fact, talking of *For the Union Dead,* but referring to the whole of Lowell's work up to that time (1964), Poirier says that what he most admires in Lowell's poems is that "they seldom invite anyone to expand inside them."

The question of whether or not one can be drawn into such hard poetry seems to be one posed by Lowell himself. Poirier feels that one is not supposed to be. At times, that is true. One is not meant to make connections. The very fact of his work-table is supposed to remain that; it is not supposed to suggest the labor and passion of Christ, as it might have in another man's poem. But, as Christopher Ricks says, one is continually being drawn in; one keeps finding new layers of context and allusion; "in its relating of the internal and the external, as of the personal, the political and the historical, 'For the Union Dead' is one of the finest poems Lowell has written"; and because of this, we are, at times, made to remember that because a poem is "both then and now, that nuclear war has indeed given us all one neck."

One thing that both Poirier and Ricks could agree on is that Lowell's allusiveness is a problem. Because Lowell makes us feel the same uncertainty we feel in a moment of life (How much does it mean? How much are we in fact involved? Can we excuse being indifferent to this?), many men will find his work oppressive. In a lazy age, his books may lie uncracked on the shelves, while critics talk easily in terms laid down before, in our own time.

Certainly another such subject for debate would have to be Lowell's conception of history. It is at once curiously personal, and blatantly Roman; Juvenal is one of his favorite Latin writers. Jarrell, Poirier, and Ricks would all agree that Lowell's present contains an enormous amount of the past; in fact, Robert Brustein finds this to be Lowell's major contribution to the modern American theater.

Always, in each of these mysteries which Lowell himself has created, we feel ourselves carried back to one thing: the text. Close textual analysis is essential, with Lowell, and, as Poirier points out, one of the signs of Lowell's originality is that he demands an entirely new kind of investigation. Anthony Ostroff's symposium on the "Skunk Hour" is a good example (see bibliography) because that is one of Lowell's important poems, and because all three of the participants are eminently well qualified to undertake this kind of study. And, as Lowell himself says, "I can't imagine anything more thorough than Nims's stanza-by-stanza exposition. Almost all of it is to the point. I get a feeling of going on a familiar journey, but with another author and another sensibility. This feeling is still stronger when I read Wilbur's essay. Sometimes he and I are named as belonging to the same school, what *Time* Magazine calls "the couth poets." Sometimes we are set in battle against one another. I have no idea which, if either, is true. Certainly, we both in different ways owe much to the teaching and practice of John Crowe Ransom. Certainly, his essay embodies and enhances my poem. With Berryman, too, I go on a strange journey! Thank God, we both come out clinging to spars, enough floating matter to save us, though faithless."

Lowell has come on a long journey since his earliest poems were published in the *Kenyon Review* in 1939. Irvin Ehrenpreis gives us an excellent summary of the over-all career of the poet, up to *For the Union Dead.* Joining those who see the early poems as strained and postured, he sees the conflicts, the irrational organization, the rebelliousness of the early poems as the struggle of a young man trying to find his voice; he sees the translations and imitations as an attempt to find a voice of his own; and in *Life Studies,* Ehrenpreis feels, Lowell at last found his language and his subject. Of course, the earlier poems hover over one's shoulder, all through *Life Studies* and *For the Union Dead,* but essentially, all our critics would agree that there was some major change here, and that it is in the poetry itself and therefore must be considered. As Ehrenpreis implies, the stubbornness of the verse, seeming to resist the reader one moment and then ensnare him the next; the vastness of the public themes and the closeness of Lowell's private view; Lowell's memory, Lowell's violent demandingness, above all, Lowell's intelligence—these elements of his verse take on new depth, as each new book comes out. That quality of growth, then, and of expansion; the deepening of his cunning, and at the same time, the strengthening of his nerve; the feeling that when Lowell suffers now, it means a good deal more than it did twenty-five years ago—these are aspects of the phenomenon of his poetry, aspects which continually provoke critics into new essays and debates. I would say, in fact, that Lowell shows one thing consistently, in all of his verse from the very beginning: Robert Lowell intends above all to be remembered. And that has made him grow. If he keeps writing poetry like this, he will be remembered. For he has managed to set our minds spinning, he makes us wonder about what he has said. We are never sure, with Lowell, just where he stands. But more important than this is the tone of voice that we hear in almost all of the poems saying, in a way, "I am trying to pack the utmost amount of meaning into the minimum of words, I expect each word to be read, carefully. I mean what I say." Just what it is he has said is unclear. But the fact is there: we do hear, in the very words of the poem, that he is trying to talk to us. This justifies a certain amount of clarification, I think. And many would say it makes the apparent confusion complex, and the conflict a battle within each one of us. Perhaps, then, exploring Lowell and life, criticism may be of some small help to us despite its fondness—and ours—for simplicities, and poetry.

After all, all writing is an attempt at communication; and, despite the fact that most criticism has a fondness for simplicity, it has, too, when it is human, a fondness for poetry, and for people, as well. Our very lives move constantly from conclusion to mystery, and back again: only the words of the poem remain constant. Having read the words, and the words about words, we must always go back, at the last, to the individual speaker, in this case, Robert Lowell, and his most considered speech, to find out what he has to tell us, about life, and, we ourselves, following him, must express ourselves as best we can: The best poetry is, after all, a perfection of speech.

New York University, 1971   JONATHAN PRICE

TABLE OF IMPORTANT DATES

1917	Robert Lowell was born on March 1, great-grand nephew of James Russell Lowell; descendant of General John Stack (Revolutionary War), Edward Winslow (puritan founder), and Major Mordecai Myers (see *Life Studies*); and distant cousin of Amy Lowell.
1935	Graduated from St. Marks School, where he had been encouraged by Richard Eberhart.
1935-1937	Harvard College.
1937-1940	Kenyon College, where he knew Allen Tate, John Crowe Ransom, and Randall Jarrell.
1940	Graduated from Kenyon *summa cum laude* in Classics; entered Roman Catholic Church; married Jean Stafford, author of *Boston Adventure*.
1940-1941	Taught English at Kenyon.
1941-1942	Editorial Assistant with Sheed and Ward, New York.
1942-1943	Fellowship to Louisiana State University, where he knew Cleanth Brooks and Robert Penn Warren, then editing *The Southern Review*.
1943	Jailed for failure to obey the Selective Service Act, after opposition to Allied bombing of civilian populations in Europe. Released after five months of a year-and-a-day sentence.
1944	*Land of Unlikeness* printed, Cummington, Massachusetts.
1946	*Lord Weary's Castle.*
1947	Pulitzer Prize for *Lord Weary's Castle;* American Academy of Arts and Letters Prize; Randall Jarrell's article "From the Kingdom of Necessity" appeared.
1947-1948	Received Guggenheim grant, and appointed Consultant in Poetry, Library of Congress.
1948	Divorced from Jean Stafford in June.
1949	Married Elizabeth Hardwick.
1950	Faber and Faber brought out *Poems: 1938-1949* in England, establishing Lowell's international reputation.
1951	*Mills of the Kavanaughs.*
1959	*Life Studies*, for which Lowell won a National Book Award.
1960	Ford Foundation fellowship to work as poet-librettist with the Metropolitan Opera and the New York City Opera. *Poesie di Montale: Con Uno Studio di Alfredo Rizzardi e un Acquerello di Morandi*, Serendipity Press.
1961	*Imitations*, which won the Bollingen Translation Prize. *Phaedra and Figaro*, with Jacques Barzun.
1964	*For the Union Dead.*
1965	*The Old Glory*, winner of the Obie Award as Best Play for 1964-65 season, after production of *My Kinsmen, Major Molineux* and *Benito Cereno*, under the direction of Jonathan Miller.
1966	*Near the Ocean.*

1967   *Prometheus Bound* produced at Yale, under the direction of Jonathan
            Miller; printed in New York *Review of Books.*
1968   *The Old Glory* printed. *The Voyage and other Versions of Poems by
            Baudelaire.* Lowell shares editing of *Randall Jarrell: 1914-1965.*
1969   *Prometheus Bound* printed. *Notebook of a Year: Nineteen Hundred Sixty-
            Seven to Nineteen Hundred Sixty-Eight.*
1970   *Notebook: Revised and Expanded Edition.*

IRVIN EHRENPREIS

The Growth of A Poet

FOR AN age of world wars and prison states, when the Faustian myth of science produces the grotesquerie of fall-out shelters, the decorous emotion seems a fascinated disgust. After outrage has exhausted itself in contempt, after the mind has got the habit of Dallas and South Africa, the shudder of curiosity remains. Every morning we think, something new and insufferable is about to happen: what is it? Among living poets writing in English nobody has expressed this emotion with the force and subtlety of Robert Lowell. In an undergraduate poem Lowell described himself as longing for the life of straightforward beliefs and deeds, of simple lust, conventional faith and boyish sports. But 'sirens sucked me in', he said; and painful, feverish contemplation was his fate:

> On me harsh birches, nursing dew,
> Showered their warm humidity.
> ('The Dandelion Girls')

Like Baudelaire, he saw things so disturbing that they almost kept him from making them into poetry.

Yet the confident life of public action might have seemed young Lowell's certain destiny. For his family line ran about as high as an American genealogy could go. His mother was descended from Edward Winslow, a Pilgrim Father who came to America on the *Mayflower*. Edward's son was a mighty Indian killer and a governor of Plymouth Colony. Lowell's mother also traced herself to the New Hampshire frontiersman John Stark, who was made a colonel at Bunker Hill and a general in the Revolutionary War. Lowell's father, though trained as a naval officer, belonged to the intellectual family that produced teachers and clergymen as well as fighters. The original R.T.S. Lowell, five generations ago, was also a naval officer. Another namesake, Lowell's great-grandfather, 'delicate, sensitive, strangely rarefied', was a poet best known for a ballad on the relief of Lucknow, and spent four years as headmaster of St. Mark's, one of the most fashionable boys' schools in the United States. Lowell's great-great-uncle, James Russell Lowell, a Harvard professor and one of the famous poets of his era, became ambassador to the court of St. James's. For most of the memories on which Lowell was bred, Puritan New England, especially Boston, provided the setting; and in the history of the Massachusett's Bay Colony he could find his Tree of Jesse.

It was on these very elements that he was to turn his first great storm of poetic disgust. They supplied the object of a clamorous repudiation. The shape the outburst took, however, depended less on ancestry than on a set of experiences that seem to have determined Lowell's original literary colour: his meeting with the circle of John Crowe Ransom and Allen Tate, his conversion to Roman Catholicism and his dramatic response to the second world war.

At St. Mark's School, Lowell found his interest in poetry encouraged by the poet Richard Eberhart, one of the teachers. He began experimenting with free verse but soon switched to stanzaic forms. As an undergraduate at Harvard he went to see Robert Frost, bearing a 'huge epic' on the First Crusade. The great man perused a page, told the visitor that he lacked 'compression', and read him Collins's 'How Sleep the Brave' as an example of something 'not too long'. For a period Lowell tried to write simple, Imagistic poems like those of W. C. Williams; but the university around him seemed less than a nest of singing birds, and he heeded a recommendation that he should study under John Crowe Ransom. In the middle of his undergraduate career, after a summer spent with Allen Tate, he left Harvard altogether and went to Kenyon College, in rural Ohio, where Ransom was teaching.

For a while now, Lowell even lived in Ransom's house, and later shared lodgings with two·other young writers, one of whom, Peter Taylor, has published a short story based on their college friendship ('1939'). During these years, the critic Randall Jarrell taught English at Kenyon, and he too lived a while with the Ransoms. It seems obvious that the network of literary affiliations gave the young student, who had been growing 'morose and solitary' at home, a welcome substitute for blood relations who felt small sympathy with his talent. Lowell often describes himself as belonging to the 'second generation' of the Fugitives; he spent long periods in a quasi-filial or fraternal connection with three or four of the authors he met in the years before the war, and he speaks of them with the sort of loyalty one extends to kin. The conservative politics, strong but orthodox religious faith and high literary standards to which these Southerners were attached must have seemed to him seductive alternatives to the commonplace Republicanism, mechanical church-going and materialist aspirations that characterised a 'Boston' formed (as he saw it) by successive lines of Puritans, Unitarians and low-church Episcopalians. To Lowell the home of his forebears stood for a rootless but immobile sterility.

In 1940, when he took a step towards establishing a family of his own, Lowell not surprisingly married another writer, the novelist Jean Stafford, whose 'flaming insight' he commemorates in a recent poem. He was also converted to Roman Catholicism, the church peculiarly associated in Boston with the large population descended from humble Irish immigrants, natural enemies, in politics and culture, of his own class. But the poet already felt committed to a kind of moral vitality that could for only a limited time be expressed in Roman terms. During the period when his new-found church was something defiant of the Boston he had repudiated, and so long as the language, symbols and ritual represented materials to be conquered and employed for explosive purposes, he could use Catholicism as an ingredient of poetry.

But when it was only the faith he had to accept, the church came to seem as oppressive and self-contradictory as the code of his native class.

It was during the years of his first marriage and his adherence to the church that Lowell's earliest books of poetry appeared. Apart from what had come out in an undergraduate magazine, the first poems he published were a pair in the *Kenyon Review* 1939. But years went by before any successors could be seen in print, partly because the few he wrote were rejected when he sent them out. Then in 1943 about a dozen of his poems turned up in the literary quarterlies, to be followed the next year by a collection, *Land of Unlikeness*. This gathering, withholding and sudden releasing of his work is typical of the poet's method; for he labours over his poems continually and plans each collection as a sequence, the opening and closing poems in each making a distinct introduction and conclusion, and the movement between them tending from past to present, from question to resolution, from ambiguous negation to hesitant affirmative.

Above the influences of Ransom and Tate, or the steady use of Catholic religious imagery, or the many motifs drawn from Boston and New England, the most glaring feature of Lowell's two earliest volumes was a preoccupation with the second world war. Not long after the United States joined that war, he committed the most dramatic public act of his life. Characteristically, this act seemed at once violent and passive, and was calculated to make his parents very uncomfortable. In what turned out to be no more than preliminary steps, he twice tried to enlist in the navy but was rejected. Soon, however, the mass bombing of non-combatants shocked his moral principles; and when he was called up under the Selective Service Act, he declared himself a conscientious objector. Rather than simply appear before the responsible board and declare his convictions, he refused to report at all, and thus compelled the authorities to prosecute him.

In order to give his deed the widest possible significance, he released to the press a thousand-word open letter to President Roosevelt. Here Lowell drew repeated attention to the historic eminence of his ancestors. He described himself as belonging to a family that had 'served in all our wars, since the Declaration of Independence', he told the President that the Lowell family traditions, 'like your own, have always found their fulfillment in maintaining, through responsible participation in both civil and military services, our country's freedom and honor'. He said that he had tried to enlist when the country was in danger of invasion but that this danger was past, and the intention of bombing Japan and Germany into submission went against the nation's established ideals. He could not participate in a war, Lowell said, that might leave Europe and China 'to the mercy of the U.S.S.R., a totalitarian tyranny committed to world revolution'.

Twenty years later he was still signing open letters of protest to newspapers; and although his opinions had altered, their direction had not shifted. 'No nation should possess, use, or retaliate with its bombs', he wrote in a 1962 symposium. 'I believe we should rather die than drop our own bombs.' It is suggestive of the poet's sensibility that he should link suicide with mass murder, as though the way to prevent the second might be to commit the first. The themes of self-destruction and assassination are often joined in his work, the one apparently redeeming or proving the altruism of the other. Yet parricide becomes a mythical, guilt-ridden route to justice and liberty; for by throwing over the traditional family pieties, the young Lowell seems to have felt he was destroying his begetters and oppressors.

The poems that appeared in *Land of Unlikeness* (1944) were mostly written during a year Lowell spent with the Tates after leaving Kenyon College. In them he devoted himself mainly to a pair of themes reflecting recent history. One was the unchristian character of the Allies' role in the second world war; the other was the causal connection between the doctrines of America's founders and the desolate condition, spiritual and material, of the country in the thirties. Looking back, Lowell saw in the ideals and motives of his ancestors the same contradictions, the same denial of a Christ they professed to worship, that made his own world a land of unlikeness, i.e. a place obliterating the image of divinity, a culture where the old metaphors that made created beings recall their creator, no longer operated. Those who had flown from persecution came here to persecute the red men; those who hated war made war on nature, plundering whales and neighbours for unspiritual profit.

In order to dramatise and generalise this view, he drew parallels between divine and human history: between the war and Doomsday, between the dust bowl sharecroppers and Cain. And he set up antitheses: between profits and mercy, between political slogans and charity. To the second world war he opposed Christ. In the social and political theories of the Fugitives, Lowell found support for his tendency to identify degeneracy with the city, the machine and Roosevelt's centralised democracy, even as he associated true civilisation with rural, aristocratic society. And since the South itself was yielding to the rapid movement from one set of conditions to the other, Lowell could apply his argument to humanity in general, through parallels drawn from *Genesis* and *Revelation,* from the myth of Troy, and from history. Thus the advent of cosmopolitan industrialism becomes a sign that we are all descended from Cain; the first Eden becomes a symbol of that ante-bellum, ostensibly Augustan society which the North supposedly destroyed; the fall of Troy becomes the analogue of the defeat of the South. Since the new war had the effect of speeding the hated process, it was easily drawn into this aspect of Lowell's rhetoric.

By the time he composed these poems, Lowell had given up free verse and was writing obscure poems in metre in a style of his own. Most of those in *Land of Unlikeness* are savagely ironical. Besides employing puns or conceits repeatedly and with great earnestness, he brought in hackneyed phrases and common tags of quotations, giving sarcastic new directions to their meaning. He invented grotesque metaphors, such as 'Christ kicks in the womb's hearse'. Although the stanzas of most of the poems are elaborate, the rhythms are heavy, the sounds are cluttered, alliteration occurs often and unsubtly. Into such verses he pressed enough violence of feeling to stun a sensitive ear. Certain dramatic monologues and visionary pieces on religious themes make the greatest uproar. The tighter the stanza forms, the wilder the bitterness: erratic rhythms, blasphemous images, deliberately hollow rhetoric erupt over the objects of his onslaught. But instead of the tight form providing an ironic contrast or intensifying counterpoint to the violent tone, it seems arbitrary. The mind that follows the form seems cut off from the mouth that screams the sacrilege:

> In Greenwich Village, Christ the Drunkard brews
> Gall, or spiked bone-vat, siphons His bilged blood
> Into weak brain-pans and unseasons wood. . . .
>
> ('Christ for Sale')

In another poem the speaker is a slum mother apostrophising the corpse of her baby, who has died on Christmas Day, 1942 (soon after the sinking of the British aircraft carrier *Ark Royal*):

> So, child, unclasp your fists,
> And clap for Freedom and Democracy;
> No matter, child, if Ark Royal lists
>   Into the sea;
> Soon the Leviathan
> Will spout American.
>
> ('The Boston Nativity')

In this kind of satire the irony sounds so wild that most readers ignore the poet's meaning while observing his frenzy. The caricature of the nativity scene does not succeed in mocking America's moral pretensions during the war. It only forces upon one's perceptions the distorted religiosity of the writer. After all, by Lowell's own argument, there could be no real heroes in history apart from Christ. As in Tate's 'Aeneas at Washington', the Southern gentlemen comes finally to seem less like Hotspur than like Richard II, standing for ideals he did not die to defend.

Yet not every speech is a tantrum. In a few of the poems Lowell's detachment suggests that his churnings, in the others, are an effort to produce a heat wave in a naturally cold climate. Observation, dry and wry commentary, fascinated disgust—these are the marks of his subtler self, and these are what appear, for example, in 'The Park Street Cemetery'. This poem, a survey of the tombstones in a Boston graveyard, has less violence than distaste in its tone. Lowell treats the site as a repository of those Puritan colonists who bequeathed to the America they founded their own confusion of grace with fortune. The form is appropriately relaxed: three stanzas, each of seven unrhymed, irregular lines; and the poet ends not with a scream but a deadnote:

> The graveyard's face is painted with facts
> And filagreed swaths of forget-me-nots.

The positive doctrines of *Land of Unlikeness* seem less significant than the negative directions. Whether Lowell espouses Southern agrarianism or Roman Catholicism, his principles attract him less as ideals of aspiration than as possibilities disdained by his ancestors. Against early New England the real charge he makes is that it failed to meet its own ultimate standards; for Lowell is after all another sober moralist with a Puritan's severity. He scolds Boston as Blake scolded London: for the death of vision and the death of conscience. Nowhere does he imply that dogma bestows serenity, or that, as some Southerners would argue, the integrity of a ceremonious traditionalism outweighs the human misery on which it may rest.

For the poet, finally, the real problem remained unsolved. In most of this volume his best-integrated poems were his understatements; those that showed the highest technical ambition were bathetic. He had to find a style that would reconcile his interest in technique with his interest in justice, that would identify private with public disturbances. For such a style the elements lay not in the regularity of his stanzas, not in the depth of his piety, and not in his political judgments. It lay in Lowell's preoccupation with tone, in his humanitarian conscience, and in his sense of history. When he employed these to enlarge the meaning of an immediate personal experience, he produced the best poems in *Land of Unlikeness:* 'The Park Street Cemetery', 'In Memory of Arthur Winslow', 'Concord' and 'Salem'.

Not only the older writers belonging to the circle of Ransom and Tate but also several other critics gave unusual attention to *Land of Unlikeness.* It was praised briefly but intensely by F.W. Dupee and Arthur Mizener. There was a careful review by Blackmur and a eulogy by J. F. Nims. But when Lowell's next book *Lord Weary's Castle* appeared (1946), the critical reception became a thunder of welcome.

As usual, there is a link between the old work and the new. In the last poem of *Land of Unlikeness* the poet had mentioned the curse of 'exile' as the alternative to the blessing of Canaan: God offered Israel the choice, says the poet; and when Israel chose to turn away from God's 'wise fellowship', the outcome was Exile. The opening poem of *Lord Weary's Castle* is called 'The Exile's Return', suggesting a common theme for both books. But the theme has broadened. In the new collection the poet implies that nothing was or could be settled by the war. In rejecting divine leadership, it is moral justice, the creative principle bringing order out of chaos, that we have banished from its selfmade home. Thus if the expatriate is taken to mean Christ, the lord still waits for the world he built to pay him his due homage. He still menaces us with the judgment that the war prefigured. As a creator, however, the Exile is also the poet or artist; and in this sense he wants to be paid for the truthful visions with which he has blessed an ungrateful world. For he holds out the threat of a poet's curse, and his isolation remains the mark of society's misdirection. In a private extension of this sense the Exile is Lowell himself, released from jail after serving about five months of the year and a day to which he had been sentenced. Coming back to ordinary routines, he meets in new forms the same moral issues he had wrestled with before his imprisonment.

All these implications are in 'The Exile's Return'. Here, an émigré comes back to his German home after the war, under the protection of American garrisons. But the shattered place looks the opposite of Eden; and if the first springtime brings lilies, it brings as well the agony of responsibility. To suggest the aspect of the neglected artist, Lowell crowds the poem with allusions to Mann's Tonio Kröger, who stood 'between two worlds' without feeling at home among either the bourgeoisie or the artists. To suggest the themes of heaven and hell, he has seasonal references to an infernal winter, a spring of rebirth, the 'fall' of autumn, and the entrance·to Dante's hell. For the motifs of imprisonment and release he uses a jail-like hôtel-de-ville, a Yankee 'commandant' and a parcel of 'liberators' who are as yet innocent or 'unseasoned'.

In direct contrast, the closing poem of the book, 'Where the Rainbow Ends', deals with an American city, Boston, that has never been bombed but that faces the dissolution caused by decay of conscience. Not war but winter devastates this city. Not as a refugee but as a voluntary exile from worldliness, the poet-prophet offers his people the alternative to the Judgment prefigured by the cold season:

> What can the dove of Jesus give
> You now but wisdom, exile? Stand and live,
> The dove has brought an olive branch to eat.
> ('Where the Rainbow Ends')

Repeatedly in this book, Lowell shows an understanding of how his elemental powers might be fused, how his unnatural calmness of tone in dealing with horrifying material might be supported by an apparent casualness of style screening a meticulous exactness of underlying structure. His sense of the past justifies ironically the calmness of tone. For to the degree that one considers human misery and cruelty as the reflection of permanent instinct—rather than transient ignorance—one will view one's own corruption and one's neighbour's not with scandalised outbursts but with comprehending calm. Furthermore, through the distancing effect of history, as through the shaping effect of complex form, one can even achieve a coherent grasp of one's own deepest, most secret anguish. With these several powers Lowell also made good use of a set of influences that he had earlier felt only at some remove, as they were present in the work of Tate, Eliot and Ransom. These influences emanate from the great line of French Symbolists and post-Symbolists, to whom the 'modern' experimental movement in poetry owes its origin. When Lowell turned to Rimbaud, Valéry and Rilke for models, he was accepting the cosmopolitan conception of literature that American poets as diverse as Whitman and Pound have worked with.

The defect of *Lord Weary's Castle* is the same as that of *Land of Unlikeness*. In Whitman, Tate and Hart Crane, one cannot help noticing a habit of substituting rhetoric, in the form of self-conscious sublimity, for poetry. If Lowell, their heir, yields to this habit, it is because, like them, he has the

highest conception of the poet's task. But the mere posture of soaring, the air
of prophecy, does not make a speech either noble or prophetic. In Lowell's most
commonly overpraised work, 'The Quaker Graveyard', the use of rhetoric joins
with a denseness of symbolism to make a poem that seems more impressive
for aspiration than for accomplishment.

Throughout this poem he contrasts two views of saving grace: the idea of
a special gift to the elect, and the idea of something that infuses not merely
all men but all creatures. The in-group's complacency Lowell attaches to the
Protestant sects of colonial New England and to his patriotic cousin, who died
at sea for a cause Lowell rejected. As a measure of the limitations of this ethic,
which he associates with war-loving capitalism, Lowell invokes the great
evolutionary chain of created beings. The world, he keeps saying, exists as a
moral order in which separate men are not masters but participants: both the
sea slime from which we rose and the whale that we plunder lie beneath the
same law that subsumes humanity. To sectarian arrogance he opposes the
innocence of the humbler orders of creation, for whom cruelty is an accident
of their nature. As the solvent of arrogance he offers the Catholic compassion
of Christ embodied in Mary his mother.

In Lowell's usual manner, the end of the poem recalls the beginning. We
move back to the Quaker graveyard on Nantucket Island off the coast of
Massachusetts. But where the initial scene was of violent death in a great war,
the closing gives us the lifeless cemetery of wind and stone and tree. Now the
poet glances back to the very start of the evolutionary process and contrasts
that moment, when life and death were born together, with the present outlook
of a corpse-littered sea. And suddenly the capacious cemetery of the Atlantic
becomes a symbolic contrast to the filled graveyard of the Quakers: God has
more room than this; the old covenant has given way to the new gospel.

In this fascinating work the failure of the rhetoric grows obvious if we notice
the weakness of the poem's penultimate section. Here Lowell puts the snug,
familiar salvation that his cousin might aspire to beside the Catholic vision of
the universal but quite unknowable God reflected in the image of Our Lady
of Walsingham. Though this passage is a deliberate understatement, the effect
is not powerful by implication; rather, it sounds bathetic. Beyond human griefs
or joys, says the poet, the Virgin

> knows what God knows,
> Not Calvary's Cross nor crib at Bethlehem
> Now, and the world shall come to Walsingham.

If we compare Lowell's two stanzas, in their attempt to express the inexpress-
ible, with similar passages in Eliot's 'Dry Salvages' (which is, with *Lycidas,* one
of the models for this poem), we must admit that there is a posed air, a willed
simplicity, in Lowell's lines that never appears in, say, 'Lady, whose shrine
stands on the promontory', etc. This forced tone seems the more regrettable
because Lowell's passage is meant to deliver the positive alternative to the
errors he denounces with such thoroughness. It is in the overcharged stretches

of churning sounds, eruptive rhythm, and violent imagery that we seem to hear the authentic voice of the poet:

> In the great ash-pit of Jehoshaphat
> The bones cry for the blood of the white whale,
> The fat flukes arch and whack about its ears. . . .

We cannot help feeling that he enjoys his destructive vision in a way not compatible with his role as prophet, moralist or recipient of wisdom.

In another long poem, 'At the Indian Killer's Grave', Lowell gives a more appropriate display of his powers. The history of its composition reminds us of his habitual alteration of his own work; for much of the poem comes out of the 'Park Street Cemetery', and the closing lines are a magnificent adaptation of verses from another early poem. Moreover, as he transforms these materials, the poet enlarges their meaning. Like the speaker in Tate's 'Ode to the Confederate Dead', the poet here contemplates a graveyard where his direct or spiritual ancestors are buried among their peers. Unlike Tate's speaker, however, he searches for the meaning of their sins, not their virtues. Staring about at the figures carved on the gravestones among the vegetation, he contrasts the Puritan dead with the living Irish who now hold political power in Boston. The sound of a train stopping underground makes him think of time stopping and of the Judgment to come; and he wonders about the fate of the Pilgrims' souls. He imagines the spirit of the Red Indian chief, King Philip, addressing the Puritan Indian-killers and reminding them that all their pretensions to being the chosen of God have left them only the corrupted bodies that now serve as carrion for sea-gulls. He looks at the toothed railing, thinks of dragon's teeth, and ponders the double source, natural (i.e. Cadmean) and spiritual (i.e. Adamic), of our instinct for evil. Then in a sudden, astonishing close, the poet turns from the old law to the new, from Adam to Christ; and he calls on the four evangelists to guide him towards the inclusive faith of the Roman Catholic church, to a vision of salvation that more than admits the Indian chief; for it promises Philip that the blessed Virgin herself will deck out his head with flowers:

> John, Matthew, Luke and Mark,
> Gospel me to the Garden, let me come
> Where Mary twists the warlock with her flowers—
> Her soul a bridal chamber fresh with flowers
> And her whole body an ecstatic womb,
> As through the trellis peers the sudden Bridegroom.

And there, in a fine identification of his private conversion with both the history of Massachusetts and the religious or mythical account of all human history, Lowell brings his poem to a close.

Generally, the poet sounds a tone of self-restraint, of calm but engrossed repugnance, that reminds one of Ransom's poems 'Necrological' and 'Arma-

geddon'. This tone he drops appropriately in two counterbalanced passages: the
outburst of Philip, who speaks with a savage violence of sound and image, and
the lyric close and climax, when calm is replaced by rapture. The apparently
loose-knit free associations rest on a carefully adjusted underpinning. Even the
setting of the poet's meditation belongs to his subject, because the Puritan
colonists brooded hourly upon death and the grave. They dressed in black and
regarded the beauties of animate nature as bad diversions from the proper study
of man, viz. death and judgment, heaven and hell. Nevertheless, they proudly
gave themselves the title of the elect of God, promoting themselves to Paradise.
It is a tremendous historical irony that their haughty Calvinism should have
given way, in Boston, to the avowedly humble, Catholic faith of the Irish—to
the church that in colonial times proselytised among the Indians instead of
beheading them. In effect, the whore of Rome waltzes over the Puritan graves:
'the trollop dances on your skulls'.

A shimmering elaboration of imagery in the Symbolist manner connects the
past and the present, the beginning of the poem with the end, the surface and
the meaning. As the poet questions the spectacle before him, he wonders
whether the fate of the dead is knowable or whether the pagan idea of
vengeance may not be carried out, so that Philip may eternally scalp the
self-styled righteous men (Blake's 'just man') who killed his people. This
scalp-head-skull image appears again and again in the poem, reaching its most
brilliant transformation at the end, when the Virgin is pictured as twisting
Philip's 'warlock' or pigtail with flowers. Between these points the head
becomes the English crown, responsible for building King's Chapel—a motif
that opposes King Charles to King Philip. It then turns into the 'dome' of
the Statehouse that replaced the royal authority. Next, Philip's head reappears
on a 'platter' or gravestone. The phrasing recalls St. John and therefore the
apostle or evangelist Philip. As a prophet now, the Indian can address his
damned enemies and point out that the Catholics are raised over their heads.
The dome becomes a globe that is the natural world, rejected (so says the poet)
by the Puritans as they 'hurled/Anathemas at nature'. The head reappears in
the headstones of the graves and finally in Mary's handling of Philip's head.

Parallel to these metamorphoses move the images of the garden. We start
in the desolate garden of the cemetery, which the Puritans have reached in place
of Paradise. Shrubs and sculpture remind one of similar scenes. So the view
expands into both the Public Garden, where the Beacon Hill brahmins walked,
and the Boston Common, which was more likely the playground of the Irish.
Lowell toys with the ironies implicit in 'garden' and 'common', and with the
further irony that though fashionable Beacon Hill is where his own class live,
it is topped by the Statehouse that in effect belongs to the Irish. Under the
Common, meanwhile, runs the subway, analogue of hell, with its serpentine
green trains, symbolic of time. Easily enough, the Garden and the Common
expand into the whole 'land' that the Puritans denounced and despoiled. This
contracts at once into the mud that buries them now. The buildings around
the Common are like palisades around the early settlements, intended, however,
not to keep the wilderness from swallowing the villages but to keep, as it were,

the remnant of natural ground from spreading. Finally, the motif reminds the poet of the ground in which Cadmus sowed the dragon's teeth, emblematic of original sin.

It seems remarkable that while some of the best poems in *Lord Weary's Castle* were imitations, or free English versions, of works in other languages, some of the least effective were dramatic monologues. In a poem like 'The Ghost', based upon Sextus Propertius, Lowell performed a superb job of giving his own voice to another poet. But in the double-monologue 'The Death of the Sheriff', the structure of which depends upon changes of voice and shifts in point of view, the speaker's smothered, crowded, dull murmur hardly alters from beginning to end. It's as though Lowell had too much to say to be able to submerge himself in an imaginary personality, and for that very reason found it easy to submerge a sympathetic author's character in his own.

His next book, *Mills of the Kavanaughs* (1951), brought these complementary tendencies to a crisis. The unqualified successes in it are a dazzling pastiche of Virgil and an adaptation of Werfel. But the longest and most ambitious works are five attempts at narrative dramatised through monologue. In four of these one feels that the poet has contrived situations offering the greatest opportunities for allusiveness and symbolism, and has sacrificed to such opportunities the absolutely essential narrative line upon which any dramatic monologue depends. He had obviously worked with immense pains over the title poem, running to more than five hundred lines, many of them beautiful evocations of the Maine landscape that gives the piece its setting. Nevertheless, although the plot would sound irresistibly sensational in summary—dealing with the madness and suicide of a patrician Catholic who married his sister by adoption—the poem is so hemmed in by cross-references and correspondences as to be wholly static. At one point Lowell goes so far as to match the number of a figure on a bird guide, once memorised by the protagonist, to the number of the stanza in which the man tries to recall the bird's name. The same substitution of arbitrary parallelism for narrative drama almost makes an impasse out of the last poem in the book, 'Thanksgiving's Over'. Here Lowell sends his main characters to a church on Thirty-First Street in New York, and situates their home next to the Third Avenue elevated train ('El'), in order to supply allusions to the Trinity.

Yet 'Thanksgiving's Over' is one of the most revealing of Lowell's poems. Published two years after his divorce from Jean Stafford and the year after his marriage to the essayist Elizabeth Hardwick, it comes from a time when he no longer felt buoyed up by the church. Louise Bogan called the book *Mills of the Kavanaughs* a 'dark midpoint' in his development, 'which must in some way be transcended'. In this closing poem Lowell shows that he was passing the midpoint and going on. All the ingredients of his false rhetorical style are here: the monologue, the nightmare, madness, murder, suicide and blasphemy. But the implications are not the old ones.

To the speaker of the poem Lowell gives the voice of a man who has lost the struggle to maintain his Christian faith and now ponders the events that culminated in his failure. He is a Roman Catholic, a New Yorker and a widower, whose young, demented wife had believed herself impregnated by the Holy Ghost. After she tried to kill herself by jumping from a window, he sent her to a sanatorium in the mountains of Vermont, where she died. It is now Thanksgiving Day, 1942, and Michael the widower half remembers, half dreams of his dead wife. As he tries to make sense out of the monstrous experiences, he thinks he hears her talking.

The themes of the wife's increasingly disconnected chatter are love and peace, her assumption being that these are united in the church. But as her incoherence deepens, it becomes clear that the serenity she offers is available only to those who are as credulous as children. Within the wife's character, therefore, the themes are split so as to suggest the opposition between religious doctrines and human nature. She would like to feel love as spiritual charity, and therefore denies her passionate impulses. She would like morality to issue from the passive acceptance of authority, and so she denies the need for a struggle between the good and evil in our constitution. Through suppression, her hidden passions become adulterous lusts projected on other persons. Towards Michael her affection turns to jealousy, and she feels like killing him. When this wish is thwarted, the hate turns inward, and she tries to kill herself.

The poet implies that by giving up religion one might resolve some of these conflicts, but one would then have to face the pain of a life without ultimate meaning. Michael must choose between abandoning God and abandoning his rational conscience. As the peculiarly shocking symbol of his dilemma the poet focuses on the doctrine of the Trinity. Thus the action of the poem is set at the very end of the Trinity season, the week before Advent Sunday. Since the third person of the Trinity appears iconographically as a dove, there is a profusion of sacrilegious bird imagery. In order to involve other aspects of doctrine or ritual, the poet complicates the central theme with allusions to the Eucharist (etymologically 'thanksgiving'), the Incarnation (as enacted in the Annunciation), and so forth. As a kind of parody of each, he produces natural analogues. Within the fantasy of the girl's unconscious the Trinity takes the form of a love triangle. She confuses the Dove with a celluloid parrot and imagines herself pregnant with birds. Since the conventional dish at an American Thanksgiving dinner is a turkey, the poet can introduce grotesque ambiguities signifying the sterility of the Holy Ghost or the end of Michael's belief: 'My fowl was soupbones.'

In flying from adultery to death, the girl was impelled by a guilt due to religion. So against the ideal of sexless conception displayed in paintings of the Annunciation, the poet sets the pagan fertility of 'St. Venus' in Botticelli's Primavera. Against the child's sexless world of faith (evoked by allusions to Mother Goose rhymes, nursery tales and Peter Pan) he sets the world of parenthood. In a distortion of phrases from the *Messiah* we hear the solution that Michael cannot yet accept: birds singing, 'Come unto us, our burden's light'—not the Dove but the birds of nature, of light and Lucifer and reason.

Over such themes the poet builds his characteristic sort of towering edifice; for the poem stands on an amazing reticulation of allusions. *Paradise Lost,* for obvious reasons, is continually evoked. The wretched couple are identified with Faust and Gretchen or with Hamlet and Ophelia: From her asylum window the wife sees the harpies of Baudelaire's 'Cythère'. Yet the essential image and meaning of the poem do not hinge on such clues. Michael sits and listens at the end of the poem, but he does not pray or receive a sign. It seems certain that when he boards a train, it will take him away from 'this deaf and dumb/Breadline for children'—as the wife unintentionally describes Roman Catholicism for the poet.

In Michael we confront again those linked themes of passive observation and wild impulse to travel that underlie so much of the nightmare violence in Lowell's poems. The wife's confinement in a cell reflects Michael's emotional seclusion. For the faithful Christian, life is a cage from which he escapes to Life; for the fallen Christian the limits of mere life make another kind of cage. Afraid to stir, for fear of wrecking the object of his stirring, the poet repeatedly speaks as a walled-off voyeur frantically watching the lives of others. Like a traveller in a sealed railway car, he passes over the earth, looking but never doing, always on the move and never in motion: he has replaced action by vision.

Lowell has said it was hard for him to find a subject and a language of his own. He can describe himself as writing a rather formal style coming out of Tate, Hart Crane, Ransom and Eliot. But when he composed the brilliant, influential poems that were collected in *Life Studies* (1959), he took a line less reminiscent of those masters than of Pound. At last he had discovered his language and subject.

By the time this book appeared, Lowell had received enough prizes and awards to ease most men's desire for public recognition. He was the father of an infant daughter (born January, 1957); he was a member of the Boston University Department of English; and he held the honorary degree of Doctor of Letters. Yet he had suffered a deeply disturbing experience when his mother died (February, 1954); and the emotional pressures evident in his poetry had undermined his health until he was forced to turn for aid to hospital treatments.

The continuance of the emotional strains, tempered by domestic amenities and balanced by extraordinary marks of success in his career, seem to have enabled Lowell to discover the best uses for his talent. Superficially the transformation appeared in the lightening of his style. Lowell has said that soon after the *Mills of the Kavanaughs* came out, the pace of his writing slowed almost to a halt, and his allusive, rhetorical manner came to seem 'distant, symbol-ridden and wilfully difficult'. He felt that his old poems too often hid what they were about, presenting a 'stiff, humourless and even impenetrable surface'. So he began paraphrasing Latin quotations when he used them, and adding extra syllables to lines in order to make them clearer or more colloquial. With such a poem as the short, perfect 'In the Cage' (1946)—a tetrameter sonnet recapturing the grimness of the months he spent in jail—he had already shown the strength of a comparatively unadorned language, free from obscurities but suffused with irony. This manner now became not the exception but the rule.

Line after line, in poem after poem, reads like a well-turned but easily spoken remark made by a fastidious, self-critical speaker who is at home with slang.

But the ease of language was only the outer sign of Lowell's new attitude towards his own nature. Without losing the tone of fascinated disgust, he now found it possible not only to treat himself as part of history but to treat history as part of himself. The course of his life became the analogue of the life of his era; the sufferings of the poet became a mirror of the sufferings of whole classes and nations. It was not as a judge that he now claimed his authority: it was as the heroic artist, the man capable of turning vision into act. Through the title of his book Lowell gave himself the status of a craftsman who reveals life in general by the rendering of his own life.

Appropriately enough, *Life Studies* opens with a train journey from the city of priests to the city of artists, Rome to Paris. But the speaker is neither a character in a dramatic monologue nor an impersonal commentator. He is the poet talking about his own experiences. Here as generally in the book, Lowell has of course invented facts and altered truths. Yet the reader feels himself in touch with the real author and not with a mask. Similarly, the entrance into the poem is deliberately casual, with what look like random associations suggesting the real flow of a unique consciousness.

If the formal frame is thus a common earthly journey, the object presented is a miraculous one: the bodily assumption of the Virgin, proclaimed as dogma in the jubilee year 1950. So the title 'Beyond the Alps' means not only a trip towards France but also its opposite, 'ultra-montane', or the old epithet for supporters of papal infallibility. Lowell is using that doctrine, which the proclamation of the new dogma pressed to a record-breaking extreme, as the emblem of vulgar human credulity—the decay of imagination into superstition—a principle embodied in the pope. To escape from such tempting corruptions, the poet struggles within himself, during the night of his train journey, emerging at dawn into a sense of rebirth, a commitment to the creative imagination. Turning towards the intellect and the arts—towards Athene and Apollo—he rejects Mary and Pius. The pope is depicted, with grotesque irony, between a purring electric razor in one hand (the cat of rational science) and a canary in the other (the dove of faith).

In keeping with the opposition between religion and art, Lowell treats the mountains that appear in his poem as versions of Parnassus. So the journey recalls the celebrated simile, in Pope's *Essay on Criticism,* comparing the Alps to the challenge that art sets before the ambition of genius: 'Hills peep o'er hills, and Alps on Alps arise.' It is thus appropriate that at the time the poem opens, the inartistic Swiss should just have failed to climb Everest.

Violence, as usual in Lowell's work, accompanies the polarity of stillness and movement. By mentioning the Swiss (historic mercenary soldiers), the poet hints at the third principle of human nature which the poem deals with, i.e. destructive violence, personified by the warrior-king. The success of Caesarean terror in chaining the mind differs only in mode from the success of the magician-priest: Mussolini is as Roman as Pius. For an ideal culture, that could make violence, magic, and reason work together, Lowell offers not Rome but inimitable Hellas; and while the morning sun, like the imagination, transforms the bleak moonlit peaks into dazzling Parthenons, the reborn poet thinks of another traveller, Odysseus, escaping symbolically from the dark cave of Polyphemus by blinding the cyclops with a dazzling firebrand. Athene, the guide of Odysseus, easily united in herself all the roles to which popes and dictators aspire; the reader recalls that she was also *parthenos* or virgin, born miraculously without a mother, inspirer of a temple outshining St. Peter's; and Lowell reminds us that she sprang not from the flesh but from the intellect of Jove. To this white height the poet dare not attempt to climb. Only Paris is left, the 'black classic' city of our own disintegrating culture; for our age seems unable to give direction and purpose to the primeval, irrational violence of human nature.

The intellectual design of this exhilarating poem has little system about it. Yet the texture, phrasing and versification offer immediate pleasures to the ear. It consists of three sonnets with slightly irregular rhyme schemes, the last of the three ending in a couplet that also serves as epigrammatic close to the whole work.* This pattern is enriched by a fullness of alliteration, assonance and internal rhyme that, so far from obtruding upon the offhand casualness of phrasing, only seems to deliver an ironical counter-thrust to it. Puns and other witticisms supply an elegant distance from which the poet can regard his own discomfort:

> I envy the conspicuous
> waste of our grandparents on their grand tours—
> long-haired Victorian sages accepted the universe,
> while breezing on their trust funds through the world.

The imagery has the same sort of forceful inconsequence: mountains and birds, tyrants and feet reappear in startling transformations as the wonderfully managed tone deepens from humour to bitterness to sublimity. The elaborate manipulations of height and depth, white and black, the four elements, are old habits of the poet. But the similar treatment of tiny details turns accidents into beauties. Thus the train stewards' tiptoe walk (while they ritually bang on their dinner gongs in a startling allusion to the Mass) becomes, in the second stanza, the toe of St. Peter, superstitiously kissed by pilgrims; and then, in the third, the splendour of the dawn of our culture as the poet sees

> Apollo plant his heels
> on terra firma through the morning's thigh.

It is not easy to overpraise *Life Studies*. I suppose the most startling ingredient in the book was the new direction taken by the poet's conscience. In place

---

* When Lowell revised this poem for his most recent collection, he also restored a fourth stanza which was judiciously omitted from the text in *Life Studies*.

of either direct protest or the fusion of his own morality with that of a Christian community, Lowell attached himself to several classes of heroic victims: children, artists, imprisoned criminals, and the mentally ill. Though these have always been linked in the Romantic tradition, most poets dealing with them risk the dangers of posturing and sentimentality. Precisely through making his own case the central case, Lowell avoids either fault. Instead of merely seeing him, we see his view of his peers.

Thus by reviewing his early memories not as they point inward but as they revolve about this or that pathetic adult, he gives a toughening perspective to the sufferings of the child; for these are balanced by the sufferings the child either causes or ironically ignores in the adult. Dealing with poets, he secures a similar distance by balancing the ignominies of the external life against the victories of the imagination. When he handles his most recalcitrant material, the humiliating lives of psychotics, he can allow himself a comical irony that would sound intolerable coming from anyone but the inmate of an institution:

> There are no Mayflower
> screwballs in the Catholic Church.
>
> ('Waking in the Blue')

Of course, each of these figures also stands as a measure of the disorder in society: the unrewarded artist, the corrupted child, the madhouse that mirrors the world. Each further becomes an extension of the past: thanks in part to the mere movement of decades, Lowell can bestow on personal recollections the dignity of history:

> These are the tranquillized *Fifties,*
> and I am forty.
>
> ('Memories of West Street')

Not through the public aspect of his ancestry but through the independent private experiences of the struggling poet, he can serve as the record of his age, and connect that age with the sweep of earlier epochs.

In all these accomplishments the controlling factor is a matter of tone. If Lowell had not managed to infuse the despair of his disgust with the humour of his irony, he could not have established the framework that screens the reader from the simple pathos of most confessional verse. In the production of this tone, the use of slang, re-sharpened clichés and witticisms is crucial: instead of straining, as in Lowell's earlier work, to give the banalities of life a moral urgency (often without succeeding), they now suggest the speaker's mastery of his experience. It is this saving irony, energised by disgust, that carries him across his most difficult, self-destructive nights. When he emerges from the darkness of 'Skunk Hour', the penultimate (originally the last) and almost the finest poem in this almost uniformly splendid book, what supports him and us is surely the power of his tolerance and humour, shoved smack up against a hideous crisis.

In tracing Lowell's career up to 1960, one may describe it as following two successive motions. When he wrote his earlier works, the poet tried to give them importance by starting from the great moral issues or crises of history and then matching those with themes derived from his private ordeals. After *Mills of the Kavanaughs,* however, he was willing to start from his private experiences and project these upon history and public life. Since the effect of the change was a fresh and distinctive kind of poetry, Lowell seems to have felt impelled to push his explorations further. Preoccupied as he was with the continuity of his own work, and educated as he was in Eliot's idea of literature as a body of classics that the innovator alters and enlarges, Lowell naturally looked around among established masters to find either foreshadowings of his discoveries or parallels to his themes and tone.

From the very beginning he had in a sense been doing this. When he incorporated other men's lines into his own verses, when he made a Latin, French or German author's words the basis for a new poem in American English, he was suggesting that at least in certain corners of their *œuvre* the strangers shared his moods. As if to show there were no limits to his ambition, Lowell now set about discovering his own qualities in the whole range of European literature. Having projected his experiences as a human being upon the history of the twentieth century, he now projected his identity as an artist upon the meaning of 'poetry'; for he began producing free adaptations or 'imitations' of the work of a dozen and a half poets from Homer to Montale. Even before they were reprinted in the collection entitled *Imitations* (1961), these poems were received with a surprising degree of incomprehension, which was aggravated rather than lightened when the whole book came out. Only the rare reader either observed that the arrangement of the book was not chronological, or accepted the author's statement that the contents were a sequence rather than a miscellaneous collection.

In fact, of course, *Imitations* is Lowell's attempt to find his voice in the high places of literature, to fashion retrospectively a tradition for his accomplishment. He is legitimising his progeny, replacing the Lowells and Winslows by Baudelaire, Rimbaud and Rilke. In drawing up such a genealogical tree, Lowell again implies that he has found his essential identity not in a social class or in a religious communion but in his character as a writer. So it seems appropriate that the bulk of the models belong to the Symbolist tradition. For Symbolism is the movement that defined the creative mind as the supreme object of poetic contemplation.

Once again, the opening and closing poems have special significance. Lowell begins with a startling extract from the *Iliad,* which picks up the motif of his 'For the Union Dead'—the last poem (under a different title) in the revised edition of *Life Studies.* 'For the Union Dead' had dealt with the mystery of heroism, in which a human life reaches nobility by the manner of death: 'man's lovely/peculiar power to choose life and die'. To open *Imitations,* Lowell gives us 'The Killing of Lykaon'. Suddenly Homer is not the Olympian whose view shifts with dignified ease from Greek side to Trojan, or from man to God; but he is the singer of the 'mania' of Achilles. 'Mania' rather than the conventional 'wrath', says Lowell in his version of the epic invocation. No doubt he is punning on *mênin,* the first word in the first of all our poems. However, he is also, and quite fairly, discovering in the ancient poet his own tendency to regard any irresistible passion as a sort of madness. The extract that follows the bit from the invocation comes from Book XXI of the *Iliad,* and contrasts heroic murder with ignominious death: Achilles insists on despatching the vanquished Lykaon and spurns his victim with a tirade on the killing of Trojans. The hero, foreseeing the dissolution of his enemies' corpses, suggests that the reduction to nothingness eliminates their value as persons. Lowell makes the speech his own by infusing it with a love-hate hysteria that sounds feverish and self-conscious but possesses a marvellously nervous vitality:

> You too must die, my dear. Why do you care?
>
> . . . . .
>
> the dark shadows of the fish will shiver,
> lunging to snap Lykaon's silver fat.

The answer to Achilles' debasement of the human spirit is the final work in *Imitations,* 'The Pigeons', from Rilke. In the middle of this poem we meet a band of Greek warriors about to die. But here they personify the poet's army of creative impulses, destroyed through being realised. The word 'mania' appears too, in the last line of the poem and the book. Yet it is no longer Achilles' rage to annihilate; it is now the resistance of reality to the artist's drive towards perfection; for the imagination of course opposes itself to nothingness and aspires to eternity. So the metaphor changes, and a poem becomes a ball flung from 'all-being' towards eternity, 'almost out of bounds', but gaining a tragic intensity, or 'body and gravity', from the pull that draws it back towards non-existence. In the exquisitely phrased first half of this fine work, Lowell-Rilke employs not a ball or an army but the flight and return of pigeons as a metaphor for the artist's impulses. Each bird is like a creative vision seeking independent life. So the most beautiful pigeon is always the one that has never left the coop, the pure conception not yet embodied; for to be fixed is to be finished. Nevertheless, says Lowell,

> only by suffering the rat-race in the arena
> can the heart learn to beat.

The soaring unity, in such lines, of slang, passion and insight reveals the strength of Lowell's talent.

The progress from the death-bounded battles of Achilles to the tragic campaigns of the artist reaches its peripety in the poems from Baudelaire, placed ironically after Hugo's tributes to the defeated warrior Napoleon and the dead artist Gautier. In Baudelaire the great themes of *Imitations* surge together: death, love and art. Lowell has selected poems that carry us from the revulsion of the artist against passion to the welcome the artist gives death.

If his style sounds drier than Baudelaire's and less felicitous in rhythm than Pound's, it has a decorous violence of language and imagery that no other American poet can produce. Yet not intensity of expression alone but strength of intellect, the consciousness enveloping the intensity, draws the disruptive forces together. Lowell's confident metres, the bold, catchy phrases, express not simply what Baudelaire felt but what we still want: a power to transcend lust and decay by the imagination that digests them:

> reptilian Circe with her junk and wand. . . .
> Desire, that great elm fertilized by lust. . . .
> It's time. Old Captain, Death, lift anchor, sink!

If in artistic sensibility Lowell seems peculiarly at home with Baudelaire, he seems as a person still more at ease with Rimbaud, whose work is placed at the exact centre of the book. With both poets he finds continual opportunities for employing his own tone and his imagery of passivity eager for motion. But Rimbaud brings out attitudes towards childhood and corrupted innocence that remind us at once of *Life Studies*. Mme. Rimbaud as 'Mother' inexorably recalls Mrs. Lowell:

> she thought they were losing caste. This was good—
> she had the true blue look that lied.

So also the isolated 'poète de sept ans' brings back the 'last afternoon with Uncle Devereux Winslow'. Yet in revealing what he shares with Rimbaud, Lowell also reveals what the rest of us share with them both. The double image here has the distancing but clarifying effect that irony produces in *Life Studies*. When he gives us his amazingly fresh, rich version of 'The Lice-Hunters'—with its symmetry of disgusting perceptions, its complexity of assonance or rhyme, and its steadiness of rhythm—Lowell evokes the whole tendency of our nagging generation to inspect, regret, and enjoy emotional crises:

> He heard their eyebrows beating in the dark
> whenever an electric finger struck to crush
> a bloated louse, and blood would pop and mark
> the indolence of their disdainful touch.

From a glance at Lowell's most recent work, coming out in periodicals, one can prophesy that his next book will establish his name as that normally thought of for 'the' American poet. It will be a wide shift from the fame of Robert Frost, whom so many non-readers of poetry were able to admire along with the literary audience. Frost did many things that Lowell does not. Though unsuccessful as a farmer, he could celebrate aspects of rural life that Lowell never touches. He knew how to tell a story. He was the last important

American poet to use the old forms and the old language convincingly. If Frost endured, in the fate of his family, more frightful disasters than Lowell, he was blessed with the power of maintaining his ego against them. Yet he stood for few extraordinary or wayward ideas. His connection with literature outside the conventional English and American models was slight. It is remarkable how often his early poems are indistinguishable from the early poems of Graves or Ransom. He opened few roads that other writers could travel. No one could call Frost a poet's poet.

Lowell, on the contrary, seems determined to maintain his intellectual distinction, his subtlety, his rigorous complexity of form. What appears most astonishing about the recent work is the way old motifs persist in new transformations with deepening significance. There are the city garden, the parallels of beast with man, the bitter pathos of memory working on the fixed character. But in the new poems of private recollection Lowell inclines to emphasise the hold that history has on the present, the powerlessness of the self to resist the determination of open or hidden memories. The insatiable consciousness of the poet comments sardonically on the very self-censuring auto-analysis that produced *Life Studies.*

At the opposite extreme from the private self the poet can now draw human as well as Symbolist analogies between the terrible numbers of suffering people and his own unique experiences. 'Buenos Aires', one of his finest new 'public' poems, has the wit and clever phrasing that make lines attractive on a first reading: 'old men denied apotheosis' (i.e. equestrian statues of defunct dictators); 'Peron,/the nymphets' 'Don Giovanni'. The poet's games with expressive sound have unusual vigour—for example, a crescendo of echoes of 'air' towards the end, preparing for the name of the city that is the subject of the poem. This 'air' becomes a sarcastic pun; for foul air, miasma, 'hot air', cold fog, emptiness, seem what the place betokens. In the final line the last word, 'crowds', echoes the last word of the first stanza, 'herds', and reminds one of the likeness drawn throughout the poem between cattle and people; for it is the suffering and passivity of the humblest class that connect them with the author.

As usual, the images are what make the poem work. This time they depend on the old partners, love and war, Venus and Mars, united here by means of Peron's name *Juan,* which suggests the Don Juan legend. Lowell, disgusted by the official facade of the city, treats it as a depopulated, over-furnished opera set, which he contrasts with the off-stage crowds of the real Argentina. The opera is of course *Don Giovanni;* and the centre of the poem recapitulates history with dead generals in white marble recalling Mozart's Commendatore. Instead of the file of Don Juan's abandoned mistresses, we meet marble goddesses mourning deceased heroes; or sex and death joined in a skull-like obelisk. Instead of the great lover in hell, we hear Peron bellowing from exile, the seducer of his people.

Among these scenes the poet moves on foot in a circular path, as spectator or sufferer. He starts from and returns to his hotel, caressing inanimate statues (his muses) en route but speaking to nobody. Instead of virile love, he encounters homosexuals in a park; but like Donna Anna, though unlike Argentina, he fights off seduction. Fascinated as so often by what repels him, he sees the truth behind the scrim and delivers it to us by way of his conscience.

A similar solidity of structure and depth of implication pervade the best of the new poems of introspection, 'Eye and Tooth' and the superb tribute to his wife, 'Night Sweat'. 'Eye and Tooth', a skilful extraction of humour from despair, illustrates a truism about middle age viz. that so far from bringing us serenity, the years leave us naked; only we learn, not without some disgust, that the self can survive even the shabbiest humiliation. The poem depends on a brilliant use of the *eye-I* pun. Treating vision as memory or id, Lowell presents the voyeur poet's eye as an unwreckable showcase of displeasing memories that both shape and torment the person. The dominating metaphor is, so to speak, 'I've got something in my I and can't get it out.' Towards the end Lowell neatly ties the public to the domestic by implying that just as his readers observe his gestures with the unease provoked by their own recollections, so his familiars must in the routines of living find his condition hardly more bearable than he does:

> Nothing! No oil
> for the eye, nothing to pour
> on those waters or flames.
> I am tired. Everyone's tired of my turmoil.

Ransom once played with the idea of Lowell's becoming the Ovid or Virgil of America. But if Lowell feels drawn to themes of epic scope, his mode is neither narrative nor celebratory. For a closer parallel we must look at another epoch in another nation, at the difficult life and disquieting art of Baudelaire. Besides the fundamental similarities of their childhoods, Baudelaire during adolescence inclined like Lowell to a lonely, morose disposition; and it was in the community of artists that he found a lasting family. He was attracted to painting but not to music. As an adult he responded more intensely to city scenes than to country landscapes. In his personality he combined deep passivity with an eagerness to keep working and moving. Though he had begun writing poetry while at school, he always procrastinated about publication, working over his poems with perfectionist ardour. When he produced a book, it was no miscellaneous gathering but an organisation of separate poems into a general scheme reflecting his peculiar outlook.

Still more persuasive are the similarities in the works. Both men have the posture of a fallen Christian. Both deal rather with the horrors of passion than the pleasures of love, and treat death as more seductive than frightening. For both of them, art emerges from profound intellection, from labour, suffering, self-disgust. They build their best poems around complex images linked by connotation, and not around arguments or events. They introduce coarse, distasteful words into a style that is rich and serious. Their poems follow circular movements, with the end touching the beginning.

Their differences are obvious. Lowell's use of history is deliberate; Baudelaire clings to immediate reality. The development of Lowell's characteristic successes depends on an impression of haphazardness at the start turning into a highly wrought climax, whereas Baudelaire's surface has elegance of workmanship throughout. Lowell relies overwhelmingly on visual imagery, whereas Baudelaire appeals elaborately to sounds, and is remarkable for a synaesthetic use of smells. Rhythmically, Lowell sounds less interesting than Baudelaire.

Yet if we search still further, if we place 'Le Cygne' beside 'For the Union Dead', the two sensibilities reveal still more intimate kinship. There is the same sympathy with the wretched, the same disgust with the life that imposes wretchedness upon them, the same transformation of the city-pent poet into an emblem of the human spirit exiled from its original home. Finally, it seems important that Lowell and Baudelaire take so much of the matter of their poems from the most secret rooms of their private lives; for the true biography of them both emerges not from a tale of their friendships or families or external careers but from their works alone. The real Lowell, like the real Baudelaire, is met with in the poetry to which he has given himself altogether.

From *American Poetry*, Stratford-upon-Avon Studies No. 7 (London: Edward Arnold, 1965), pp. 69-95.

ALLEN TATE

Introduction to *Land of Unlikeness*

THERE IS no other poetry today quite like this. T. S. Eliot's recent prediction that we should soon see a return to formal and even intricate metres and stanzas was coming true, before he made it, in the verse of Robert Lowell. Every poem in this book has a formal pattern, either the poet's own or one borrowed, as the stanza of "Satan's Confession" is borrowed from Drayton's "The Virginian Voyage," and adapted to a personal rhythm of the poet's own.

But this is not, I think, a mere love of external form. Lowell is consciously a Catholic poet, and it is possible to see a close connection between his style and the formal pattern. The style is bold and powerful, and the symbolic language often has the effect of being willed; for it is an intellectual style compounded of brilliant puns and shifts of tone; and the willed effect is strengthened by the formal stanzas, to which the language is forced to conform.

A close reader of these poems will be able to see two general types, or extremes which it is the problem of the poet to unite, but which I believe are not yet united: this is not a fault, it merely defines the kind of poet that Lowell, at this early stage, seems to be. On the one hand, the Christian symbolism is intellectualized and frequently given a savage satirical direction; it points to the disappearance of the Christian experience from the modern world, and stands, perhaps, for the poet's own effort to recover it. On the other hand, certain shorter poems, like "A Suicidal Nightmare" and "Death from Cancer", are richer in immediate experience than the explicitly religious poems; they are more dramatic, the references being personal and historical and the symbolism less willed and explicit.

The history of poetry shows that good verse does not inevitably make its way; but unless, after the war, the small public for poetry shall exclude all except the democratic poets who enthusiastically greet the advent of the slave-society, Robert Lowell will have to be reckoned with. Christopher Dawson has shown in long historical perspective that material progress may mask social and spiritual decay. But the spiritual decay is not universal, and in a young man like Lowell, whether we like his Catholicism or not, there is at least a memory of the spiritual dignity of man, now sacrificed to mere secularization and a craving for mechanical order.

From *Land of Unlikeness* (Cummington, Mass.: The Cummington Press, 1944), pp. i,ii.

HUGH B. STAPLES

Land of Unlikeness

'Such is the condition of those who live in the Land of Unlikeness. They are not happy there. Wandering, hopelessly revolving, in the "circuit of the impious" those who tread this weary round suffer not only the loss of God but also the loss of themselves. They dare no longer look their own souls in the face; could they do it they would no longer recognize themselves. For when the soul has lost its likeness to God it is no longer like itself: *inde anima dissimilis Deo, inde dissimilis est et sibi;* a likeness which is no longer like its original is like itself no more.'[1]

—Etienne Gilson, *The Mystical Theology of St. Bernard.*

Land of Unlikeness reflects a mind deeply preoccupied with the alienation of the human soul from the Mind of God. The title is taken from St. Bernard, but ultimately derives from St. Augustine's metaphor (*'regio dissimilitudinis'*) for the agony of a soul still held captive by the world of the senses yet sufficiently aware of God to perceive the dark strangeness of the material world and the falsity of mortal existence pursued for its own sake. The spiritual consequences of such inchoate awareness are emphasized by the book's epigraph, *Inde anima dissimilis Deo inde dissimilis est et sibi,* from St. Bernard's sermons on the *Song of Songs;* the phrase has for modern readers the suggestion of psychological schism as well. The Lowell of *Land of Unlikeness,* like the Eliot of the *Waste Land* before him, portrays the nightmare of contemporary culture, made specially vivid by the holocaust of World War II. It records the quest of a Christian for religious security against a background of chaos, disorder and destruction.

In the twenty-one poems of Lowell's first volume, revelation and hallucination merge. He consistently evokes the grotesque, as in 'The Crucifix', where he overcomes a mood of religious despair by rejecting Adam and his legacy of Original Sin in these terms:

> Get out from under my feet, old man. Let me pass;
> On Ninth Street through the Hallowe'en's soaped glass

1. Etienne Gilson, *The Mystical Theology of Saint Bernard* (London: Sheed and Ward, 1940), p. 58.

I picked at an old Bone on two crossed sticks
And found, to *Via et Vita et Veritas*
A stray dog's signpost is a crucifix.

The pervasive tone of these spiritual exercises is sombre and violent; the emphasis is on the Dark Night of the Soul rather than the Light of Salvation, on an awareness of Evil rather than a celebration of the power of Good. And although the ritual quality of some of the poems, reflected in such titles as 'On the Eve of the Feast of the Immaculate Conception, 1942', evidences the piety and gravity with which they are conceived, there remains a sub-stratum of doubt, an apprehension that God's patience may at last be exhausted and the promise of Salvation withdrawn. Throughout, there is a fascination, almost Manichean in its intensity, with the power of Evil. Perhaps the keynote to *Land of Unlikeness* is supplied by the frontispiece, which pictures not a conventional crucifix, but a gargoyle hanging from the Cross. The symbolism of this device, like that of many of the poems, seems deliberately ambiguous as if to suggest on the one hand the triumph of Christianity over Satan, and on the other the modern displacement of spiritual values, wherein not Christ but the power of Evil is elevated as an object of worship.

In a review of *Four Quartets*, Lowell wrote: 'My own feeling is that union with God is somewhere in sight in all poetry, though it is usually rudimentary and misunderstood.'[2] While it is true that all of the *Land of Unlikeness* poems, even the inventions on historical themes such as 'Napoleon Crosses the Beresina' and 'Dea Roma' have a religious context, the intensity and direction of religious force vary a good deal from poem to poem. As R. P. Blackmur puts it: 'in dealing with men his faith compels him to be fractiously vindictive, and in dealing with faith, his experience of men compels him to be nearly blasphemous.'[3] The greater number of these poems are impersonal and apocalyptic; they are set in a contemporary, sometimes topical framework in which the spectacle of mass destruction stands in dramatic contrast to the teachings of the Church. Some, however, dwell on earlier evidence of man's inhumanity to man drawn from the history of New England. Thus in such poems as 'Children of Light' and 'The Park Street Cemetery' (later expanded and more trenchantly entitled 'At the Indian Killer's Grave') Lowell deals not with the predicament of a world that has ceased trying to attain union with God, but with a culture even more hopelessly damned—a society that committed atrocities in the name of a false creed—the Calvinism of the Puritan theocracy. In two poems, Lowell strikes a personal rather than a professional pose: 'A Suicidal Nightmare' and 'The Drunken Fisherman', but in both cases the opportunity for purely lyrical expression is somewhat obscured by a heavy coating of melodrama; indeed, it is only in his latest poems in *Life Studies* that personal experience is recorded with clarity and frankness. All three of these subjects—the gloomy lamenta-

2. *Sewanee Review*, 51 (Summer 1943), 432.
3. R. P. Blackmur, *Language as Gesture* (London: Allen and Unwin, 1954), p. 362.

tions over the world conflict, the satiric probing of the spiritual malignancies
in the history of New England, and the exploitation of personal anguish, are
integrated in only one poem, 'In Memory of Arthur Winslow'. This elegy to
his grandfather is the finest of all Lowell's early poems and merits a full
discussion later in this chapter.

For Lowell, the war seems to have been Armageddon; to his poetic vision,
as to Blake's, the appurtenances of an industrial civilization are accommodated
directly into a general allegory: bombers become destroying angels, warships
are Leviathans. Cain and Abel, Adam, Mars, Bellona, Satan and even the Virgin
appear as contenders in the cosmic field while the issue hangs in doubt. In his
personal career, Lowell's attitude towards the war ranged from vain attempts
to enlist to an obdurate defiance of authority that ended in his imprisonment.
Something of this ambivalence is felt in the dozen religious interpretations of
the hostilities: their difficulty owes as much to a lack of consistent viewpoint
as to the unexpected application of allusion and the curious air of colloquial
intimacy with which the mythological and divine antagonists are addressed.
Thus it is sometimes impossible to separate Lowell's anger and despair from
his irony and satire.

In the opening stanza, for example, of 'On the Eve of the Feast of the
Immaculate Conception, 1942', the attempt to yoke the Virgin with Mars and
Bellona seems to be a satiric indictment of Christian militancy, and the odd,
shocking epithet 'burly' reinforces the apparent mood of bitter jest:

> Mother of God, whose burly love
> Turns swords to plowshares, come, improve
>   On the big wars
> And make this holiday with Mars
> Your Feast Day, while Bellona's bluff
> Courage or call it what you please
>   Plays blindman's buff
>   Through virtue's knees.

Yet the poem goes on to deplore the Virgin's failure to intercede in the
hostilities. Citing the medieval tradition of her victory over Satan, the poet
invokes her aid in these pungent terms:

> Oh, if soldiers mind you well
> They shall find you are their belle
>   And belly too;
> Christ's bread and beauty came by you,
> Celestial Hoyden, when our Lord
> Gave up the weary Ghost and died,
>   You shook a sword
>   From his torn side.

> Over the seas and far away

They feast the fair and bloody day
When mankind's Mother,
Jesus' Mother, like another
Nimrod danced on Satan's head.
The old Snake lopes to his shelled hole;
Man eats the Dead
From pole to pole.

The language here reflects in part a young poet's conscious striving for novelty; it is barely rescued from bathos by the dignity and strength of the religious emotion that produced it. In these poems, the quasi-facetious manner is usually balanced by the sincerity of the poet's faith. This kind of contradiction is likewise demonstrated in 'The Boston Nativity', in which Lowell attacks the empty, decadent 'unchristian carollings' sung by Beacon Hill revellers on Christmas Eve:

'Peace and goodwill on earth'
Liberty Bell rings out with its cracked clang.
If Baby asks for gifts at birth,
Santa will hang
Bones of democracy
Upon the Christmas Tree.

Yet surprisingly the poem ends on a note of faith that counteracts the earlier tone of cynicism:

Jesus, the Maker of this holiday,
Ungirds his loins' eternal clay.

A similar contrast is developed in 'The Bomber'. After picturing the Bomber as a symbol of *hybris,* the poet prophesies mankind's impotence in the Day of Judgment, an event always imminent in *Land of Unlikeness:*

O Bomber your wings are furled
And your choked engines coast.
The Master has had enough
Of your trial flights and your cops
And robbers and blindman's buff
And Heaven's purring stops
When Christ gives up the ghost.

In the remainder of the war poems, 'Scenes from the Historic Comedy', 'The Crucifix', 'The Wood of Life', 'Christmas Eve in the Time of War', 'Cistercians in Germany', and 'Leviathan', Lowell's partisan enthusiasms are modified by his insistence on seeing the human conflict as of minor importance. The events taking place around him are merely reflections of the greater cosmic conflict;

international warfare is viewed as a footnote to the story of Cain and Abel; military disasters are rehearsals for the impending Day of Judgment. In a sense, Lowell implies, human history does not matter any more—perhaps God has his mind on larger matters.

Under the surface decoration of these poems, behind the ritual and the conventional symbolism, lies the agony of doubt. The petitions to the Virgin, the religious meditations, the assertions of faith are shot through with an obsessive blood-guilt. And on a formal level, the intricate patterns contrast with the tone of violence and the disruptive force of blunt, clanging imagery; indeed, this central conflict between order and destruction lends these poems their chief distinction. For example, in 'Dea Roma', Lowell begins in an easy, Audenesque conversational manner which heightens the violence of his theme:

> Augustus mended you. He hung the tongue
> Of Tullius upon your rostrum, lashed
> The money-lenders from your Senate House;
> Then Brutus bled his forty-six percent
> For *Pax Romana*. Quiet as a mouse
> Blood licks your Greek cosmetics with its tongue.

The device, though effective, is a perilous one; occasionally the force of Lowell's indignation bursts through even the most severe metrical restraints; the effect is no longer colloquial, but desperate and breathless, as of a man shouting at the top of his lungs. Thus, in 'Christ for Sale', no amount of carefully premeditated rhyming can rescue his indictment of religious exploitation from prosaic vulgarity:

> In Greenwich Village, Christ the Drunkard brews
> Gall, or spiked bone-vat, siphons His bilged blood
> Into weak brain-pans and unseasons wood:
> His auctioneers are four hog-fatted Jews.
> In furs and bundlings of vitality,
> Cur ladies, ho, swill down the ichor in this Dye.

Altogether, Lowell is trying too hard here; his disgust for the 'loitering carrion', as he calls them in his final stanza, is deeply felt, no question about that, but the total effect remains emetic rather than aesthetic. The last line in particular is a bold experiment in cacophony, but it betrays a youthful partiality for rhetorical exaggeration where restraint is needed, and a disturbing insensitivity to rhythm that is by no means completely absent in even the later work. Few poets are as uneven in this respect: often in a single poem Lowell is capable of such imaginatively rendered images as this from 'A Suicidal Nightmare':

> A wooly lava of abstractions, flowed
> Over my memory's inflated bag.

only to sink to the flat prose of the concluding lines:

'Brother, I fattened a caged beast on blood
And knowledge had let the cat out of the bag.'

Similar infelicities mar 'The Boston Nativity', 'Scenes from the Historic Co ne-
dy', and 'The Wood of Life', where the comic effect of the double-rhyr ie of

Here are scales whose Reckoning-weight
Outweighs the apple's fell dejection;
Our cornerstone, the Jews' Rejection

can hardly have been intended in this solemn celebration of Good Friday.
Again, in 'Satan's Confession', Lowell's conception of our original parent as a
kind of gross *rentier* has a certain shock value but his language is bathetic:

Adam, you idle-rich
Image of the Divine:
   Tell me, what holds your hand?
   Fat of the land.
My wife's a bitch;
My Garden is Love's Shrine

To be sure, we may overlook the offence to decorum, but when the grotesque
becomes merely farcical, the force of the poem as a whole is irretrievably
diminished.

Like Eliot and Pound, Lowell is preoccupied with a sense of loss that results
from contrasting the promise of the past to the futility of the present. The
alienation of man from God, which I take to be the central theme of all the
poems in *Land of Unlikeness,* finds its most dramatic expression for Lowell in
the failure and death of the Puritan tradition. Perhaps in 'Children of Light'
he has in mind his own ancestors, one of whom, Josiah Winslow, was com-
mander-in-chief of the colonial forces in King Philip's War:

Our Fathers wrung their bread from stocks and stones
And fenced their gardens with the Redman's bones;
Embarking from the Nether Land of Holland,
Pilgrims unhoused by Geneva's night,
You planted here the Serpent's seeds of light;
And here the pivoting searchlights probe to shock
The riotous glass houses built on rock,
And candles gutter in a hall of mirrors,
And light is where the ancient blood of Cain
Is burning, burning the unburied grain.

Lowell's use of paradox here reminds one of John Donne. By a reversal of the
normal connotations of 'light' and 'dark' he provides an ironic comment on
the parable of the unjust steward in Luke xvi ('And the Lord commended the
unjust steward because he had done wisely; for the children of this world are

wiser in their generation than the children of light'). Something too of Donne's fondness for word-play can be seen in the deliberate pun 'the Nether Land of Holland'. Again, as in many of Donne's poems, 'Children of Light' is constructed upon a central paradox. The first five lines sum up the past; they represent the pious but misguided Puritan fathers whose material hardships in the Bay Colony are paralleled by the more important failure of false doctrine to provide spiritual nourishment: they are the 'Pilgrims unhoused by Geneva's night'. The second five lines juxtapose the present, in which the crime of Cain committed by the Puritans against the Indians has become enormously magnified into the holocaust of World War II. Ironically, the force of the Founding Fathers' religious zeal has been reduced to vain and illusory ritual.[4] The single-minded pursuit of Mammon has vitiated piety; abundance has become excess and the surplus wheat cannot be consumed.

In 'The Park Street Cemetery' Lowell contrasts the bright dreams of the Pilgrim ('The stocks and Paradises of the Puritan Dracos / New World eschatologies / That fascinated like a Walpurgis Nacht') to the shabby Boston of the present, "Where the Irish hold the Golden Dome'. Similarly, the sonnets to Concord and Salem, symbols of New England's past intellectual and mercantile glory, are heavily imbued with images of paralysis and death: Concord, with its 'ruined Bridge and Walden's fished-out perch', and Salem, where 'Sea-sick spindrift drifts or skips / To the canvas flapping on the seaward panes' and 'sewage sickens the rebellious seas'. These early poems prefigure the apocalyptic destruction of Boston, the New Babylon, envisioned in 'As a Plane Tree by the Water' and 'Where the Rainbow Ends' of *Lord Weary's Castle*.

Lowell's indictment of the Protestant ethic and his portrayal of the consequences of its deterioration into mere materialism derive, then, from his general preoccupation with the spiritual vacuity of the present. His disapprobation of the things of this world and of the pagan energy of those who mistakenly pursue them finds its richest expression in the fine elegy to his grandfather, 'In Memory of Arthur Winslow'. Here Lowell displays, in a sustained effort, his astonishing ability to move with ease from the moral geography of Boston, capital of the *Land of Unlikeness,* to the cosmic scene, in which symbolism drawn from both Christian and pagan tradition are harmoniously fused.

As in many of Lowell's poems, we begin with a specific locale—Phillips House (the private, expensive division of the Massachusetts General Hospital), the Union Boat Club; in the second section, the Stark cemetery in Dunbarton, New Hampshire; Columbus, Ohio, in the third; and Copley Square in the fourth. From these still points in the turning world, there is a movement in the direction of the transcendental: from Charles River to the Acheron; from Copley Square to Heaven and Hell. But the Public Gardens, reserved in Lowell's boyhood for the *élite* are now desecrated by the 'mid-Sunday Irish'; and in 'Dunbarton' even the stones, the rocks of ages are cleft, and like the tradition they commemorate, subject to dissolution.

4. The line 'And candles gutter in a hall of mirrors' (*Land of Unlikeness*) is revised in *Lord Weary's Castle* to read 'And candles gutter by an empty altar'.

We find in Part III that Grandfather Winslow has sought for permanence in the backward look at the family's historical achievement, but his compulsion to revive the past and make it meaningful in terms of the present has only led him to pursue an *ignis fatuus:* the power of gold. In his passionate attachment to the phenomenal world, Arthur Winslow has dissipated his spiritual capacities to the point where:

> the coxes' squeakings dwarf
> The *resurrexit Dominus* of all the bells.

The language of the Vulgate remains for him literally an unknown tongue; this is the reason why the poet, in his role as mediator, puts the words from the *Miserere* (slightly altered from *me* to an inclusive *nos*) into Latin:

> Lavabis nos et super nivem dealbabor

in his effort to effect a kind of posthumous conversion. For Grandfather Winslow, the beautiful stained glass windows in the Protestant Trinity Church represent the limits of his spiritual imagination, just as they do for Villon's mother in the famous prayer he wrote for her—a ballade on which this section is based. The painted paradise symbolizes ceremony without faith, doomed to sink like Atlantis in the Devil's jaw.

Throughout the poem runs a dialectic of past and present, in which the past, or history is favourably compared to the present. Ultimately, however, the sordidness of the present vitiates even the nobility of the past. Thus in the second section, Lowell's own ancestors are rejected and subdued by 'the minister, Kingsolving'. Their day is gone; the envisioned greatness of the Puritan theocracy has not fulfilled its promise. The memory of their deeds, and their artefacts, remain as a kind of monument to misguided zeal, but their example is of no help to the living. Going further than this, in the final section Lowell, projecting his own spiritual development, tries to explain that it is precisely the operation of history, in terms of the family mercantile tradition (the 'clippers and the slavers') that has prevented his grandfather from attaining grace. The narrow limits of Calvinism, with its vision of Paradise as harps and lutes, with its doctrine of election ('Kingsolving's church' becomes 'the costly church' in the *Lord Weary's Castle* revision) has precluded the necessary apprehension of the transcendent power of God's mercy. All that is left for the poet is to pray for absolution through the Blood of the Lamb.

The final impression one retains from a reading of *Land of Unlikeness* is one of gravity. There are blemishes in these poems, nearly all of them stemming from a lack of sense of proportion. Yet Lowell's concern is cosmic; it is as though he were engaged in adapting the book of *Revelation* to a contemporary framework, and it is no wonder that the book as a whole is marked by a complete absence of humour. In its place, however, is a kind of highly intellectualized wit, a *discordia concors* that has its nearest equivalent in the Metaphysical poetry of the seventeenth century. Lowell was not content in his first volume to confine himself to mere finger exercises; on the contrary, the organ-roll is there from the very beginning. When he fails, as in 'Christ for Sale', he seems to me to fail completely, but by the same token, his successes, such as 'Children of Light', and 'In Memory of Arthur Winslow', are important achievements. In his next volume, *Lord Weary's Castle*, Lowell is to gain a greater control over the violence of his imagination, and at thirty he is to attain the maturity and insight that enabled him to write, as Randall Jarrell has said, one or two poems that will be read as long as men remember English.

From *Robert Lowell: The First Twenty Years* (New York: Farrar, Straus and Cudahy, 1962), pp. 22-31.

RANDALL JARRELL

From the Kingdom of Necessity

MANY OF the reviews of *Lord Weary's Castle* have been conscious that it is an event of the order of Auden's first book; I know no poetry since Auden's that is better than Robert Lowell's. Everybody who reads poetry will read it sooner or later. I hope that I can help readers by pointing out its distinguishing features, by tracing its development, and by analyzing the themes that unify it.

Underneath all these poems "there is one story and one story only": when this essential theme or subject is understood, the unity of attitudes and judgments underlying the variety of the poems becomes startlingly explicit. The poems understand the world as a sort of conflict of opposites. In this struggle one opposite is that cake of custom in which all of us lie imbedded like lungfish—the stasis or inertia of the complacent self, the satisfied persistence in evil that is damnation. In this realm of necessity the poems place everything that is closed, turned inward, incestuous, that blinds or binds: the Old Law, imperialism, militarism, capitalism, Calvinism, Authority, the Father, the rich who will "do everything for the poor except get off their backs." But struggling within this like leaven, falling to it like light, is everything that is free or open, that grows or is willing to change: here is the generosity or willingness or openness that is itself salvation; here is "accessibility to experience"; this is the realm of freedom, of the Grace that has replaced the Law, of the perfect liberator whom the poet calls Christ.

Consequently the poems can have two possible movements or organizations: they can move from what is closed to what is open, or from what is open to what is closed. The second of these organizations—which corresponds to an "unhappy ending"—is less common, though there are many good examples of it: "The Exile's Return," with its menacing *Voi ch'entrate* that transforms the exile's old home into a place where even hope must be abandoned; that extraordinary treatment of the "Oedipus complex," "Between the Porch and the Altar," with its four parts each ending in constriction and frustration, its hero who cannot get free of his mother, her punishments, and her world even by dying, but who sees both life and death in terms of her, and thinks at the end that, sword in hand, the Lord "watches me for Mother, and will turn / The bier and baby-carriage where I burn."

But normally the poems move into liberation—even death is seen as liberation, a widening into darkness: that old closed system, Grandfather Arthur Winslow, dying of cancer in his adjusted bed, at the last is the child Arthur whom the swanboats once rode through the Public Garden, whom now "the ghost of risen Jesus walks the waves to run/Upon a trumpeting black swan/ Beyond Charles River to the Acheron/Where the wide waters and their voyager are one." (Compare the endings of "The Drunken Fisherman" and "Dea Roma.") "The Death of the Sheriff" moves from closure—the "ordered darkness" of the homicidal sheriff, the "loved sightless smother" of the incestuous lovers, the "unsearchable quicksilver heart/Where spiders stare their eyes out at their own/Spitting and knotted likeness"—up into the open sky, to those "light wanderers" the planets, to the "thirsty Dipper on the arc of night." Just so the cold, blundering, iron confusion of "Christmas Eve Under Hooker's Statue" ends in flowers, the wild fields, a Christ "once again turned wanderer and child." In "Rebellion" the son seals "an everlasting pact/With Dives to *contract*/The world that *spreads* in pain"; but at last he rebels against his father and his father's New England commercial theocracy, and "the world *spread*/ When the clubbed flintlock broke my father's brain." The italicized words ought to demonstrate how explicitly, at times, these poems formulate the world in the exact terms that I have used.

"Where the Rainbow Ends" describes in apocalyptic terms the wintry, Calvinist, capitalist—Lowell has Weber's attitude about the connection of capitalism and Calvinism—dead end of God's covenant with man, a frozen Boston where even the cold-blooded serpents "whistle at the cold." (Lowell often uses cold as a plain and physically correct symbol for what is constricted, static, turned in upon itself.) There "the scythers, Time and Death,/ Helmed locusts, move upon the tree of breath," of the spirit of man; a bridge curves over Charles River like an ironic parody of the rainbow's covenant; both "the wild ingrafted olive and its root/Are withered" (these are Paul's terms for the Judaism of the Old Law and the Gentile Christianity grafted upon it); "every dove [the Holy Ghost, the bringer of the olive leaf to the Ark] is sold" for a commercialized, legalized sacrifice. The whole system seems an abstract, rationalized "graph of Revelations," of the last accusation and judgment brought against man now that "the Chapel's sharp-shinned eagle shifts its hold/On serpent-Time, the rainbow's epitaph." This last line means exactly what the last line in "The Quaker Graveyard"—"The Lord survives the rainbow of his will"—means; both are inexpressibly menacing, since they show the covenant as something that binds only us, as something abrogated merely by the passage of time, as a closed system opening not into liberation but into infinite and overwhelming possibility; they have something of the terror, but none of the pity, of Blake's "Time is the mercy of Eternity."

The worshiper climbs to the altar of the terrible I AM like a victim, to breathe the rarefied and intolerable aether of his union with the divinity of the Apocalypse; he despairs even of the wings that beat against his cheek "What can the dove of Jesus give/You now but wisdom, exile?" When the poem has reached this point of the most extreme closure, when the infinite grace that atones and liberates is seen as no more than the bitter and useless wisdom of the exile, it opens with a rush of acceptant joy into: "Stand and live,/The dove has brought an olive branch to eat." The dove of Jesus brings to the worshiper the olive branch that shows him that the flood has receded, opening the whole earth for him; the olive branch of peace and reconciliation; the olive branch that he is "to eat" as a symbol of the eaten flesh and blood of Christ, of atonement, identification, and liberation. Both the old covenant and the new still hold, nothing has changed: here as they were and will be, are life and salvation.

Lowell seems a strange opposite of the usual Catholic convert, who distrusts freedom as much as he needs bondage, and who see the world as a liberal chaos which can be ordered and redeemed only by that rigid and final Authority to which men submit without question. Lowell reminds one more of those heretical enthusiasts, often disciplined and occasionally sanctified or excommunicated who are more at home in the Church Triumphant than in the church of this world, which is one more state; a phrase like Lowell's "St. Peter, the distorted key" is likely to be appreciated outside the church and overlooked inside it, *ad maiorem gloriam* of Catholic poetry. In Lowell's poems the Son is pure liberation from the incestuous, complacent, inveterate evil of established society, of which the Law is a part—although the Father, Jehovah, has retained both the violence necessary to break up this inertia and a good deal of the menacing sternness of Authority as such. (It is interesting to compare the figure of the Uncle in early Auden, who sanctifies rebellion by his authority; the authority of Lowell's Christ is sanctified by his rebellion or liberation.)

Anyone who compares Lowell's earlier and later poems will see this movement from constriction to liberation as his work's ruling principle of growth. The grim, violent, sordid constriction of his earliest poems—most of them omitted from this book—seems to be temperamental, the Old Adam which the poet grew from and partially transcends; and a good deal of what was excessive in the wonderful rhetorical machine of a poem like "The Quaker Graveyard at Nantucket," which catches and twists to pieces the helplessly enjoying reader, is gone from his latest poems, or else dramatically justified and no longer excessive. "The Quaker Graveyard" is a baroque work, like *Paradise Lost;* but the coiling violence of the rhetoric, the harshly stubborn intensity that accompanies its verbs and verbals, the clustering stresses learned from accentual verse, come from a man contracting every muscle, grinding his teeth together till his shut eyes ache. Lowell's later work has moved in the direction of the poem's quiet contrast-section, Walsingham; the denunciatory prophetic tone has disappeared, along with the early satiric effects that were one of the poet's weaknesses. The later poems depend less on rhetorical description than on dramatic speech; their wholes have escaped from the hypnotic bondage of the details. Often the elaborate rhetorical stanzas have changed into a novel sort of dramatic or narrative couplet, run-on but with heavily stressed rhymes. A girl's nightmare, in the late "Katherine's Dream," is far more open, classical, and speech-like than the poet's own descriptive meditation in an earlier work like "Christmas at Black Rock." It is important to understand this development; the reviews I have read have not realized that it exists.

Lowell has a completely unscientific, but thoroughly historical mind. (It is literary and traditional as well: he uses the past so effectively because he thinks so much as it did.) Lowell's present contains the past—especially Rome, the late Middle Ages, and New England—as an operative skeleton just under the skin. This is rare among contemporary poets, who look at the past as Blücher looked at London: "What a city to sack!" (Actually he said, "What a mix-up!" But this fits, too.) War, Trade, and Jehovah march side by side through these centuries: it is the fundamental likeness of the past and present, and not their disparity, which is brought out. "Cold/Snaps the bronze toes and fingers of the Christ/My father fetched from Florence, and the dead/Chatters to nothing in the thankless ground/His father screwed from Charlie Stark and sold/To the selectmen." This is the history of New England's nineteenth century in a sentence. Lowell's period pieces, which range from Propertius to Jonathan Edwards, are notable partly for their details—which are sometimes as magically and professionally illusionary as those of "I, Claudius"—but mainly for the empathy, the historical identification, that underlie the details. These period pieces are intimately related to Lowell's adaptations of poems from other languages; both are valuable as ways of getting a varied, extensive, and alien experience into his work. Dismissing these adaptations as "translations" is like dismissing "To Celia" or "Cathay," and betrays an odd dislike or ignorance of an important and traditional procedure of poets.

Lowell is an extremely professional poet, and the degree of intensity of his poems is equaled by their degree of organization. Inside its elaborate stanzas the poem is put together like a mosaic: the shifts of movement, the varied pauses, the alternation in the length of sentences, the counterpoint between lines and sentences, are the outer form of a subject matter that has been given a dramatic, dialectical internal organization; and it is hard to exaggerate the strength and life, the constant richness and surprise of metaphor and sound and motion, of the language itself. The organization of Lowell's poems resembles that of traditional English poetry—especially when compared to that type of semi-imagist modern organization in which the things of the poem seem to marshal themselves like Dryden's atoms—but often this is complicated by stream-of-consciousness, dream, or dramatic-monologue types of structure. This makes the poems more difficult, but it is worth the price—a great many of the most valuable dramatic effects cannot be attained inside a more logical or abstract organization. Lowell's poetry is a unique fusion of modernist and traditional poetry, and there exist conjoined in it certain effects that one would hitherto have thought mutually exclusive; however, it is essentially a post- or anti-modernist poetry, and as such is certain to be influential.

Lowell is wonderfully good at discovering powerful, homely, grotesque, but exactly appropriate particulars for his poems. "Actuality is something brute," said Peirce. "There is no reason in it. I instance putting your shoulder against a door and trying to force it open against an unseen, silent, and unknown resistance." The things in Lowell's poems have, necessarily, been wrenched into formal shape, organized under terrific pressure, but they keep to an extraordinary degree their stubborn, unmoved toughness, their senseless originality and contingency: no poet is more notable for what, I have read, Duns Scotus calls *haecceitas*—the contrary, persisting, and singular thinginess of every being in the

world; but this detailed factuality is particularly effective because it sets off, or
is set off by, the elevation and rhetorical sweep characteristic of much of the
best poetry of the past. Lowell is obviously a haptic rather than a visual type:
a poem like "Colloquy in Black Rock" has some of the most extraordinary
kinesthetic effects in English, perfect duplications of what is being described.
It is impossible not to notice the weight and power of his lines—most others
look a little threadbare or transparent beside them. Because of passages like

> In the great ash-pit of Jehoshaphat
> The bones cry for the blood of the white whale,
> The fat flukes arch and whack about its ears,
> The death-lance churns into the sanctuary, tears
> The gun-blue swingle, heaving like a flail,
> And hacks the coiling life out . . .

the smooth, calm, and flowing ease of some passages, the flat ease of the
ordinary speech of others, have more than their usual effectiveness: the dead
mistress of Propertius, a black nail dangling from a finger, Lethe oozing from
her nether lip, in the end can murmur to the "apple-sweetened Anio":

> . . . Anio, you will please
> Me if you whisper upon sliding knees:
> "Propertius, Cynthia is here:
> She shakes her blossoms when my waters clear."

The poems' wit is often the wit of things: the "poised relations sipping
sherry/And tracking up the carpet," the "postgirl sounding her French horn"
over the snows of Maine, the "stern Colonial magistrates and wards/of Charles
the Second." The "corn-fed mouse/Reined in his bestial passions"; the "red-
flanneled madmen looked through bars." One laughs out in church.

Lowell, at his best and latest, is a dramatic poet: he presents people, actions,
speeches, things as they feel and look to people; the poet's generalizations are
usually implied, and the poem's explicit generalizations are there primarily
because they are dramatically necessary—it is not usually the poet who means
them. He does not present themes or generalizations but a world—and the
differences and similarities between it and the ordinary one bring home to us
themes, generalizations, and the poet himself. There is never any exploitation
of the "personality" of the poet; the I who stands meditating by Hooker's statue
or the Quaker graveyard is closer to the different I's of the dramatic monologues
than to the man who wrote them. It is partly because of this that atheists are
vexed by his Catholic views, and Catholics by his heretical ones, so much less
than they normally would be.

But there are other reasons. The poet's rather odd and imaginative Catholicism is thoroughly suitable to his mind, which is so traditional and dramatic
that no images from the sciences, next to none from philosophy, occur in his
poems. Such a Catholicism is thoroughly suited to literature, since it *is* essen-

tially literary, anthropomorphic, emotional. It is an advantage to the poet to
have a frame of reference, terms of generalization, which are themselves human,
emotional, and effective as literature. "Bodily Changes in Fear, Rage and
Hunger" may let the poet know more about the anger of Achilles, but it is
hard for him to have to talk about adrenalin and the thalamus; and when the
arrows of Apollo are transformed into "a lack of adequate sanitary facilities,"
everything is lost but understanding. (This helps explain the dependence of
contemporary poetry on particulars, emotions, things—its generalizations,
where they are most effective, are fantastic, though often traditionally so.)
Naturally the terms of scientific explanation cannot have these poetic and
emotional effects, since it is precisely by the exclusion of such effects that
science has developed. Lowell's Catholicism represents effective realities of
human behavior and desire, regardless of whether it is true, false, or absurd;
and, as everyone must realize, it is possible to tell part of the truth about the
world in terms that are false, limited, and fantastic—else how should we have
told it? There is admittedly no "correct" or "scientific" view of a great many
things that a poet writes about—values, emotions, and so forth—and he has
to deal with them in dramatic and particular terms, if he has foregone the
advantage of pre-scientific ideologies like Christianity or Marxism. (Of course
it seems to me an advantage that he almost necessarily foregoes; I remember
writing about contemporary religious poems, "It is hard to enjoy the ambergris
for thinking of all those suffering whales," and most people will feel this when
they encounter a passage in Lowell telling them how Bernadette's miraculous
vision of Our Lady "puts out reason's eyes." It does indeed.)

It is unusually difficult to say which are the best poems in *Lord Weary's
Castle:* at least a dozen are realized past changing, triumphs that vary only in
scope and intensity—a number of others are poems that almost any living poet
would be pleased to have written. But certainly some of the most wonderful
things in the book are "Where the Rainbow Ends," "Between the Porch and
the Altar," "The Quaker Graveyard in Nantucket," "Colloquy in Black Rock,"
"The Death of the Sheriff" (especially the first of the two poems that compose
it), and "At the Indian-Killer's Grave." Close to these are "The Exile's Return,"
"The Ghost," "Charles the Fifth and the Peasant," "Death from Cancer," "Mr.
Edwards and the Spider," "Christmas Eve under Hooker's Statue," "Mary
Winslow"—and I cannot leave unmentioned poems like "After the Surprising
Conversions," "The Drunken Fisherman," "The Blind Leading the Blind,"
"The Shako," "France," and "New Year's Day." I do not list a number of small
or partial successes that will delight anyone who loves poetry.

When I reviewed Lowell's first book I finished by saying, "Some of the best
poems of the next years ought to be written by him." The appearance of *Lord
Weary's Castle* makes me feel less like Adams or Leverrier than like a rainmaker
who predicts rain, and gets a flood which drowns everyone in the country. A
few of these poems, I believe, will be read as long as men remember English.

From *Poetry and the Age* (New York: Random House, 1955), pp. 250-65.

WILLIAM CARLOS WILLIAMS

In a Mood Of Tragedy

THE MILLS OF THE KAVANAUGHS. By Robert Lowell. 55 pp. New York: Harcourt, Brace & Co. $2.50.

IN HIS new book Robert Lowell gives us six first-rate poems of which we may well be proud. As usual he has taken the rhyme-track for his effects. We shall now have rhyme again for a while, rhymes completely missing the incentive. The rhymes are necessary to Mr. Lowell. He must, to his mind, appear to surmount them.

An unwonted sense of tragedy coupled with a formal fixation of the line, together, constitute the outstanding character of the title poem. It is as though, could he break through, he might surmount the disaster.

When he does, when he does under stress of emotion break through the monotony of the line, it never goes far, it is as though he had at last wakened to breathe freely again, you can feel the lines breathing, the poem rouses as though from a trance. Certainly Mr. Lowell gets his effects with admirable economy of means.

In this litle poem, a dramatic narrative played out in a Maine village, Mr. Lowell appears to be restrained by the lines; he appears to *want* to break them. And when the break comes, tentatively, it is toward some happy recollection, the tragedy intervening when this is snatched away and the lines close in once more—as does the story: the woman playing solitaire in the garden by her husband's flag-draped grave. She dreams of the past, of the Abnaki Indians, the aborigines and of how, lying prone in bed beside her husband, she was ravished in a dream.

Of the remaining five poems, "Her Dead Brother" is most succinct in the tragic mood that governs them all, while the lyric, "The Fat Man in the Mirror" (after Werfel) lifts the mood to what playfulness there is—as much as the mode permits: a tragic realization of time lost, peopled by "this pursey terror" that is "not I." The man is torn between a wish and a discipline. It is a violently sensual and innocent ego that without achievement (the poem) must end in nothing but despair.

Is the poet New England—or what otherwise is his heresy (of loves possessed only in dreams) that so bedevils him? At the precise moment of enjoyment she hears "My husband's Packard crunching up the drive." It is the poet's struggle to ride over the tragedy to a successful assertion—or is it his failure?—that gives the work its undoubted force.

Shall I say I prefer a poet of broader range of feeling? Is it when the restraints of the rhyme make the man restless and he drives through, elbows the restrictions out of the way that he becomes distinguished or when he fails?

It is to assert love, not to win it that the poem exists. If the poet is defeated it is then that he most triumphs, love is most proclaimed! the Abnakis are justified, their land repossessed in dreams. Kavanaugh, waking his wife from her passionate embraces, attempts to strangle her, that she, like Persephone, may die to be queen. He doesn't kill her, the tragedy lying elsewhere.

The tragedy is that the loss is poignantly felt, come what may: dream, sisterhood, sainthood—the violence in "Falling Asleep Over the Aeneid"; "Mother Maria Theresa"; "David and Bathsheba in the Public Garden," excellent work. What can one wish more?

From *The New York Times Book Review,* 22 April 1951, p. 6.

JEROME MAZZARO

The Mills of the Kavanaughs

IN *The Mills of the Kavanaughs* Lowell's interest in plot and character prompts seven new poems, all primarily human, time-possessed, and definite. Ranging into the "longer poem" category, they complete the disintegration of the anagogical level in Lowell's poetry and, at the same time, provide more diversification in his characterizations. The realization this his basic poetic vision relied heavily on sensuous detail, that he was unable to develop, as Dante had, a new way of looking at things, that his interest was in the active rather than the contemplative life, or that drama is basically anthropocentric rather than theocentric may account for this disintegration. In any case, the disintegration provides for the inclusion of new ideas and personages neither interested in nor capable of understanding the structure of religious contemplation. Having emerged, these voices receive a sympathy and understanding not often shown previously by the poet.

The only poems in the volume which in any way try to reverse this tendency and return to Lowell's earlier contemplative structure are "Falling Asleep over the Aeneid" and "Her Dead Brother." Both, however, in their choices of subject matter and theme merely reinforce the necessity of abandoning the form. "Falling Asleep over the Aeneid," a character poem, depicts the Lowell persona in an old man in Concord who "forgets to go to morning services. He falls asleep while reading Vergil, and dreams that he is Aeneas at the funeral of Pallas, an Italian prince." By his action, he is seeking, like the hero of "The Death of the Sheriff," to break the cycle of his existence, for he senses that he, too, must go backward to salvation. But rather than go insane, he tries to accomplish this escape through dreams. Religiously, this poem is by far the more successful of the two attempts.

Expressionistic in its distortion of the outer world and its violent dislocations of time and space, the poem images the world as it appears to the troubled mind of the hero. This world is pictured in a long interior monologue in which the hero is about to repeat in his dreams actions which immortalized his predecessor. As did "Mr. Edwards and the Spider," the poem borrows extensively from its source and presents the thoughts of the modern-day Aeneas in a paraphrase-translation from the *Aeneid.* For example, the lines, "And I stand up and heil the thousand men/Who carry Pallas," come from Book XI:

Haec ubi deflevit, tolli miserabile corpus

imperat, et toto lectos ex agmine mittit
mille viros. . . .

In the same manner, later in the poem, the following lines from Book XI:

> hic iuvenem agresti sublimen stramine ponunt
> qualem virgineo demessum pollice florem . . .
> cui neque fulgo adhuc nec dum sua forma recessit;
> non iam mater alit tellus virisques ministrat,

are rendered:

> You are the flower that country girls have caught,
> . . . the design
> Has not yet left it, and the petals shine;
> The earth, its mother, has, at last, no help. . . .

Interposed between these borrowings are references to Book IV of the *Aeneid,* which predicts this tragedy, quotations from St. Francis de Sales's *Treatise on the Love of God,* and allusions to Nietzsche.

The whole poem, a love poem, depicts the various kinds of love possible on earth. It begins with Queen Dido's thwarted, all consuming love. Against her famous curse, "First, let him see his friends in battle slain,/And their untimely fate lament in vain," it pictures a modern Aeneas repeating the farewell kiss of her sister: "I greet the body, lip to lip." The perpetual war which Dido bequeathed Rome as a consequence of Aeneas' desertion has begun, and from it hopefully there may be the founding of a new Rome.

Lowell's poem then goes on to represent other kinds of love. His description of Aeneas covering the body demonstrates love for one's fellowman:

> But I take his pall,
> Stiff with its gold and purple, and recall
> How Dido hugged it to her, while she toiled,
> Laughing—her golden threads, a serpent coiled
> In cypress. Now I lay it like a sheet;
> It clinks and settles down upon his feet,
> The careless yellow hair that seemed to burn
> Beforehand.

Like the earlier passages, it is taken from Vergil:

> tum geminas vestis auroque ostroque regentis
> extulit Aeneas, quas illi laeta laborum
> ipsa suis quondam manibus Sidonia Dido
> fecerat et tenui telas discreverat auro.

harum unam iuveni supremum maestus honorem
induit arsurasque comas obnubit amictu. . . .

The memorable Aethon section echoes Achilles' death in the *Iliad* and extends
this love to brute animals:

> Aethon, the hero's charger, and its ears
> Prick, and it steps and steps, and stately tears
> Lather its teeth; and then the harlots bring
> The hero's charms and baton—but the King,
> Vain-glorious Turnus, carried off the rest.

It, too, derives from Vergil:

> post bellator equus positis insignibus Aethon
> it lacrimans gruttisque umectat grandibus ora.
> hastam alii galeamque ferunt; nam cetera Turnus
> victor habet.

But in this war two additional kinds of love are needed: St. Francis de Sales's
love of God, especially in the bird-priest sequences, and Nietzsche's love of
spirit as Lowell asks the speaker to "try,/O Child of Aphrodite, try to die:/To
die is life." For both Nietzsche and St. Francis death is an escape from form,
a release into eternal love. As St. Francis states: " . . . this soul, who, as a
heavenly nightingale . . . , cannot at will sing the benediction of his eternal
love, . . . cries . . . deliver poor me from the cage of my body, free me from
this little prison. . . . " This liberation is what is achieved when Pallas is
compared to "A wild bee-pillaged honeysuckle brought/To the returning
bridegroom." The metaphor, God being the Eternal Bridegroom, is one which
St. Francis uses for the soul of the meditator: "In which our spirit . . . be filled,
. . . as a sacred bee, moves over the flowers of holy mysteries, to extract from
them the honey of divine love." The implied religious ecstasy of the metaphor
is the closest any figure gets to mysticism.

This discussion of love leads not to the founding of a new Rome but to the
impending death of heroism, pictured in the closing lines of the poem when
the modern Aeneas is awakened by the closing of the church services. The bells
of the church have frightened away the yellowhammers who had droned him
to sleep, and he is reminded now of his great aunt who used to scold him:
"Vergil must keep the Sabbath." Her husband, his Uncle Charles, appears
dressed in the bird-peaked uniform of the Civil War and frowned upon by
visions of Philip Brooks and Grant. He has achieved salvation by giving his
life for others. Thus, like the lovers in "The Death of the Sheriff," the hero
has only become aware of his need for salvation and cannot achieve it, committed as he is to the Apollonian traditions of his family and the tenuous make-
believe valor of dreams. In this sense the poem seems to differentiate between

Uncle Charles, who gave his life to oppose slavery, and Vergil, who merely dreams of doing something heroic. Actions, not intentions, Lowell seems to say again, are the basis for salvation, and at the same time he indicates that the present is not capable of such saving actions.

A thematic collage of several previous poems, "Her Dead Brother" introduces a pair of troubled lovers and relates the causes of the suicide of the narrator after her brother's death in war. The first section outlines the nature of their life-time cycle and the religious symbols again at work—the Lion of St. Mark, the dragon, water, and ice. Paired as opposing life-death forces, they recur at intervals throughout the narrative. Once more incest—the most primitive means of opposing the Uroboros and the perversion of love, the nature of man's soul—forms the principal device of the characters' attempted escape.

The poem opens with the stock contemplative "storeroom" imagery of the Lion of St. Mark. This lion, crested in the windows of the house, opposes the coiled, German-silver picture frame of the brother's portrait, which mirrors the dragonish sunset. The images, taken from the Apocalypse, reflect the same world-ending Apollonian state which begins "Between the Porch and the Altar," where the time-bound "Adam" was shown rummaging through similar artifacts in his mother's home, recalling the fall of Troy. As in that poem, the description ends with references to Shakespeare and Homer that convey acceptance of a contradictory Dionysian spiritism: "All's well that ends:/Achilles dead is greater than the living." Achilles, who represents for the speaker both her brother and the Dionysian, awakens her to the emptiness and futility of her present ice-house state and urges her forward into escape.

In the "garden" imagery of the second stanza, the narrator recalls the "bird-watching" summer excursions with her brother to Sheepscot and the milk-snake which he killed and which her father shellacked to the ice-house door. Later, during the memory's move into winter, she recalls the August 23 of their sin—the anniversary of the Sacco-Vanzetti execution—when their mother and her maids motored to Stowe. These recollections shape and collide in her mind, beginning to take on strange meanings when she is interrupted by the sounds of her husband's Packard crunching up the drive. The effect of these collisions is again to turn the heroes into symbolic coiled serpents.

The remainder of the poem, with the suicidal delirium of its flowing gas, describes merely, as did the previous poem, the attempt to unwind these images and find an end to the life-time cycle: "The gas, uncoiling from my oven burners, dims/The face above this bottled *Water Witch*." Occurring three months after the first episode, this part opens with the distraught sister envisioning the circumstances of her brother's death: 'The ice is out: the tidal current swims/Its blocks against the launches as they pitch/Under the cruisers of my Brother's fleet." The "Water Witch," the name of a knockabout manned by her brother and fouled in Boston Light, presents to her, in its model and echo of the past, a vessel to bring both to afterlife. Its name, indicative of the romanticism of that past, derives from a novel by James Fenimore Cooper in which a pirate captain, known as "The Skimmer of the Seas," mans a small brigantine, "Water Witch." The captain abducts a beautiful heiress, Alinda de

Barbarie, and is pursued by Alinda's suitor, Captain Ludlow. Finally, he restores Alinda to her suitor.

The poem's voyage into afterlife is more complicated and detailed than the already discarded swan-journey of "Death from Cancer." Through the earlier milk-snake image, it is linked in the sister's delirium with the ice-house. She and her brother must maneuver the yacht through the ice-flows of the harbor, where the ice, symbolizing the soul in its contained or Apollonian form, presents the main obstacle to safe passage. Heeling in the fog and being pushed by the covenant of her rainbow sail, the "Witch" pauses briefly as her winds turn mute. Then, reminiscent of "The Death of the Sheriff," the Lord appears dark, like the night with all its constellations, and the narrator goes into a frenzied ecstasy: "The Lord is dark, and holy is His name;/By my own hands, into His hands! My burners/Sing like a kettle." But quickly this ecstasy turns into hysteria when the launches she envisions come on to sink the cruisers of her brother's fleet, and the yacht dies. Afterward comes the final, quiet realization that she has not achieved the likeness of God, but the likeness of her dead brother.

The failure of both poems to achieve mystical visions results not from technique, since all the elements of the previous successful contemplative poems are present, but from the basic subject matter of the poems. In choosing the "old man in Concord" in "Falling Asleep over the Aeneid," Lowell has chosen a person interested, like Martha, in the active life, in worldly not contemplative love. Likewise, in choosing incest and suicide for the plot of "Her Dead Brother," he is forced again by the moral level of his poem to re-condemn its hero. The sister, who feels that she is approaching the true Noonday, is actually enchanted by Hypocrisy, the noonday devil. The situation echoes the one described by St. Bernard in his sermons *On the Song of Songs* in his warning of the noonday devil who often comes disguised, sometimes even as the true Noonday: "The Apostles, also, on a certain occasion when they were laboring at the oars, with the wind against them, tossing their little boat about, seeing the Lord walking upon the water and thinking it was an apparition, so that they cried out for fear—did they not betray a suspicion of the noonday devil?"

Thus, in the face of these changes in subject matter, Lowell's attempt to uphold his earlier contemplative structure results in a growing breach between style and subject matter which he tries to close by forcing his subject matter. His current concerns, reflecting those of his time-damned heroes, are not contemplative and metaphysical, but worldly and moral. Yet by dint of habit, he seems to avoid new structures which may be more appropriate to his needs. The failure of adjustment is most evident in the two plot and character poems and in the remaining poems of the volume which, as their subjects move farther from contemplation, show more clearly the separation. With their meditational structures, they come no closer to filling the gap.

Despite its title, "Mother Marie Therese," the next poem in the volume, returns to the noncontemplative meditational direction of Lowell's work. Its portrayal of a nun in the postcontemplative, active life of a Martha reveals one

temporary solution. Time, the metaphysical villain of the six previously discussed poems, is absent, for as Father Turbot observes, "N-n-nothing is so
d-dead/As a dead s-s-sister." Even the nun concludes one must "tarry a little"
and "disregard Time's wings and armor." Traditionally dead to the world, she
is wrapped in the eternal peace which most of Lowell's other characters seek.
In this peace—"chastised" to the Rule's restraint, her "worldly serpent" washed
by Christ's sweat—she has returned to the active life to await world end. But,
as St. Bonaventure points out in his *Meditations on the Life of Christ*, it is the
active life in its second stage—"in doing good actively to the neighbor
. . . as in ruling, teaching, and helping in the salvation of souls." Thus in
contrast to the heroes of "Between the Porch and the Altar" and "Her Dead
Brother," she lives her life, pictured as the demanding "émigrée in this
world and the next," without any compulsion to return to contemplation. In
her, Lowell shows for the first time both the peace of the truly Christian life
which his characters try to achieve and an acceptable means of attempting it.

Concerned with a second nun's recollection of that peace and of the Mother's
steadying hand, the poem describes a time when nuns are becoming increasingly unsettled and the chances of leading a truly Christian life are becoming more
remote. Although God's Providence has mastered them, even a "buck ruffed
grouse" finds their "stern virginity/*Contra naturam.*" Remembered for her
"strangled grouse and snow-shoe rabbits," the Mother had been a stern master
of unsettled novices before her drowning on an excursion in the Atlantic. Her
firm, aristocratic ways, representative of the uncompromising Hohenzollern
standards of her background, have disappeared, and the Order now neglects
even to pay its occasional respects. Often not up to the exacting demands of
its calling, it sees only a comparable neglect by the warring world outside,
whose aims have become the Order's opposite, self-destruction rather than
salvation: "Mother, we must give ground,/Little by little; but it does no good."
The Mother, who refused to give ground in her lifetime, is being washed by
the waters of the Atlantic for her final encounter with God.

A brilliant tribute to both the figure of Mother Marie Therese and her
calling, the poem achieves not only a certain "worldliness," but approaches in
its structure and content a degree of sympathy not previously common in
Lowell's work. Of the two levels on which it exists, neither is at variance with
the subject matter. The historical level compassionately pursues the qualities
which made the Order strong, the snuffing of crones' and cretins' fear, and the
moral level undertakes the actions of its four characters, including the Atlantic.
Both function easily and without the poet's usual resort to nightmarish and
melodramatic situation. Like "Falling Asleep over the Aeneid," they combine
into an interior monologue which, rather than being expressionistic, imitates
the stylized soliloquy of the Elizabethan stage. As a result, it comes closest of
all the poems discussed to achieving the intended dramatic moment. In these
accomplishments as well as in Lowell's new humanity and warmth, it well
deserves Randall Jarrell's tag as "the best poem Mr. Lowell has ever written."

The poem which follows it, "David and Bathsheba in the Public Garden,"
tries to present a seventeenth-century dialogue of Body and Soul and fails on

at least two grounds to equal the success of "Mother Marie Therese." Nevertheless, its attempt to develop plot and character through dialogue while maintaining some semblance of a single verse style does represent a change from
Lowell's previous structures. Presenting the Boston counterparts of the Biblical
lovers, the poem suggests an expansion of character by dealing with two actors.
This requires character delineation and variety. As realized, however, the poem
fails to provide this expansion. Both characters are extremely mannered and
allusive and seem the manifestation of a single voice. As Randall Jarrell
remarks, "They both . . . talk just like Mr. Lowell." Likewise, the poem, a
reiteration of Lowell's earlier presentments on man's unlikeness to God, fails
in its meditational structure and suffers from the same lifelessness which
marked his notional assents to vision in *Land of Unlikeness*.

Set at the start of the marriage, "David to Bathsheba" details the attempts
to make Bathsheba forget her wronged husband Uriah and assume her role as
David's wife. To the question "And he is nothing after death but ground,/
Anger and anguish, David?" he replies that he must live according to the nature
of his soul: "I lie/Drinking our likeness from the water. Look:/The Lion's
mane and age! Surely, I will not die." But the question, already posed and
answered to the poet's satisfaction in "At the Indian Killer's Grave," has an
extremely clearcut and sinister solution: At the Last Judgment, those trans-
gressed against will judge the souls of the transgressors. This is Bathsheba's
fear and her eventual conviction as the poem moves into its second part,
"Bathsheba's Lament in the Garden."

Years later David has taken a new wife, Abishag, and Bathsheba sits in the
garden again, talking to her son. Her mind rambles over the past events, and
she asks herself once more if Uriah will sit in judgment. Without David's
assurance of Divine purpose, she is troubled by what her actions have brought
about—the death of Uriah, David's new distance, and the wars which have set
David against his sons and the sons against each other. Consistent with "At
the Indian Killer's Grave," her conclusion—"I must surely die"—opposes
David's optimistic statement and ends the poem.

"The Fat Man in the Mirror," which follows, is an extremely worldly and
successful picture of a hair-bellied, dog-eyed, middle-aged man just awakening
to the fact of his condition. Taken in part from Franz Werfel's "Der Dicke
Mann im Spiegel," the poem shuns the quiet, sinister sentimentality of the
original for the hustle-bustle bravado of remembered childhood. Free of its
author's usual preoccupation with death and guilt, it is an extremely gay,
melodic song whose success as dramatic form rests entirely in a direct, lyrical,
and compassionate presentation. Its limitation is a lack of Lowell's usual
"significant" content.

With the nightmare world of "Thanksgiving's Over," this content returns.
The structure of the poem, a variation of the expressionistic structure of
"Falling Asleep over the Aeneid," follows the dream of a man whose wife, "a
German-American Catholic," leaped from the window of their apartment
before her eventual death in a Vermont sanitorium. Concerned with the death
of love in their marriage, the poem develops through a series of dialogues

between the dead woman and her sleeping husband. The technique, first used in "David and Bathsheba in the Public Garden," is aided in this instance by several factors. The wife, presented as a figment of her husband's imagination, takes on the hallucinatory aspect of a mystical experience, and Lowell can employ devices of the contemplative structure without resorting to mysticism. In addition, so presented, she need not have the character differentiation of a separate person.

The opening lines of the poem establish the world outside the room, and the noises of New York City's "El" purposely echo those of the opening lines of "Falling Asleep over the Aeneid" with their mating yellowhammers. Here "warred" instead of "mating" and "night" instead of "sun" suggest the differences between the conditions of the poems. In this poem Christ, traditionally portrayed as "light" and "love," is missing, and the world is making little effort to recover Him. Bird imagery again conveys the nature of the Christian soul, but in non-Christian surroundings the soul is liberated by insanity not death. Insanity is identified in the poem with the parrot who "possesses" the wife and who represents by his name and action "imitation" or "likeness." He is equated in the demented wife's mind with the Lord: "The Lord is Brother Parrot, and a friend."

Knowing what such birds have done to her mind, her husband Michael asks "Whose friend?" and wakens to the El's rattle as a train passes. Noticing anew the barred windows and the various bird-representations throughout the apartment, he falls asleep again. In his sleep his wife returns to tell him that before he sent her off to Vermont he committed his greatest sin by destroying her capacity for love. For this he would be damned. Meanwhile, she, in her insane world of perpetual spring and birds, traces their idyllic youthful love to the autumn when "Flocks/ Scavenge for El Dorado in the hemlocks." Protected in this world by Venus, the goddess of love, she opposes her husband, "Archangel Michael," and rapidly passes through a series of mentally warped Biblical and mythological love tales including that of Susannah and the Elders, until she finally arrives at the scene where her husband's lack of love causes her leap from the window. She describes her commitment, like the goddess Persephone's, as a winter and entreats her husband to resurrect her into spring through love. Fearing the dead as well as death, he awakens trembling from this dream and says a rosary to still their souls.

In its way, the poem opposes point for point the illustrations of love in "Falling Asleep over the Aeneid" and demonstrates by negative examples the world as it is without the understanding and humanity of one's fellowman. Love and religion are set in conflict and both suffer. Since love is the nature of the soul, the poem is one of the most horrifying that Lowell has written.

But if Lowell can exclude contemplation from the structure of his poems, he cannot exclude his interest in flights from form. "The Mills of the Kavanaughs," the last written poem of the volume and the longest that Lowell has yet published, represents his efforts to deal with the problem without returning to mysticism. A composite of techniques borrowed from poems discussed, it opens with a woman sitting in her garden with her Bible, "Sol," playing solitaire, and recollecting her life. With its "rut of weeds that serpents down a hill" and its Apollonian image of Persephone, the goddess of immortality, the life in the opening stanza suggests the recurrence of the problem which plagued many of Lowell's characters, the archetypal Uroboros. Against that suggestion Anne Kavanaugh, armed with "Sol" and dressed in dungarees, represents a new type of heroine to meet the situation. Her husband Harry, the namesake of a line of English kings and heir to the Kavanaugh tradition as well as protector and restorer of the Kavanaugh properties (an old family mansion in Damariscotta Mills, Maine), recalls the other heroes who have died opposing time. To them he adds the imaginary lover, the destructive guilts, the withdrawals, and at times even the description found in Jean Stafford's story of marital dissolution, "A Country Love Story," suggesting perhaps a common biographical incident from their marriage linking the story, this poem, and a later poem, "The Old Flame." This possibility is further strengthened by the Kavanaugh motto: 'Cut down, we flourish." The motto is that of Lowell's maternal ancestors, the Winslows.

The history of the Kavanaugh tradition, currently being destroyed by time and taxes, is outlined in the second stanza. While playing cards Anne briefly traces the events which made her Mrs. Kavanaugh and placed her in this garden. Her first recollection is her first visit as a trespasser to the peaceful Kavanaugh world. Then, too, she had "queened" it. Now, brought back to the present by the pool's statues, she admonishes her dead husband for having given up too quickly and is reminded in turn by "Sol" that her "gambling with herself/Is love of self." She thinks of Daphne, who was so in love with herself that she resisted the advances of the sun-god Apollo. "Sol," who represents in a way the new sun-god and her salvation, must not be so thwarted. Absorbed in these thoughts, she forgets that her husband is dead and tries to call him. But just before she does, she realizes what has happened and returns to her game, recording her score on another time image, "the Life/Insurance calendar." She is struck by the implication and jests: "Sol, . . . Sol,/If you will help me, I will win the world." In response, she sees only a young boy blowing dandelion pollen in the air and her thoughts wander off again.

This time, together with Harry, she returns to spring and the pagan rites of regeneration and immortality suggested by the symbol of the pollen. These rites are sensual and animalistic and so are the images which follow. Her dog, worrying "through the coils of the brush," returns the Uroboros image. He is pursued by memories of a "pileated bird" who with his bill once killed sandsnakes in the flotsam and of children, especially Anne, caught in the circling whirlpool and rockpools of the river.

It is through Adam's sin, however, that they entered the lifetime cycle, and it is through Jehovah, not Zeus, that they must achieve salvation. She understood this and should have conveyed it to Harry in their marriage. In failing to do so, she has killed a part of herself. To regain this part as priestess of salvation, her mind returns her to a world turned Avernus, where, seeing herself as a new Persephone, she tells of her escape from the Hades of her childhood. Adopted by the Kavanaughs, she grows up on their estate and eventually falls

in love with Harry. On their wedding night, aware of their responsibility to
the past, they vow to restore the woods of Kavanaugh to their children. This
vow proves meaningless, and her mind telescopes through the guilt-ridden,
childless years of their marriage to Harry's retirement from the Navy. Having
failed to accomplish either the restoration of the woods or the generation of
their line, they spend this retirement, the whole of World War II, at home,
viewing the empty countryside at harvest. Thus, she has failed in her simplest
function as priestess of salvation, as the means of bodily regeneration suggested
by the boys and the dandelion pollen. As a result, Harry is dispirited and she
tries vainly to revive him.

Christmas, for Christians the time of the birth of the Redeemer, portrays
Harry caught up by the same forces—family tradition—which damned "Adam"
in "Between the Porch and the Altar." The snow outside is being cleaned by
a snowplow which as "a clowning dragon" again evokes the serpent-Uroboros
image. That night, Anne dreams that she is having an affair with another man.
Through her garbled dream utterances, Harry realizes the situation and tries
to kill her, thinking the man is real. He recovers in time, only to have his mind
permanently affected. She faints and dreams a second time. Afterward, his body
and mind, depressed by failures, degenerate, while she pampers him ineffectual-
ly through the spring and summer.

Autumn again, and the new Persephone returns to Hades. She dreams that
her luck at cards—like Orpheus' lute—has brought back her husband from the
dead, thus breaking his life-time cycle and bringing him into immortality. In
her mind she celebrates this, then awakens and tries anew to summarize the
Kavanaugh achievements, seeing in the distance the room where Harry's
mother worked to save the mills. She explains that even in religion she has
failed: "He died outside the church/Like Harry Tudor." She is ashamed that
they spent so much of their lives attempting to escape death and wonders, at
their failures, why: "Why must we mistrust/Ourselves with Death who takes
the world on trust?" Her answer lies in a complete acceptance of death: "And
for no other reason, Love, I gave/Whatever brought me gladness to the grave."
Thus like Daphne who escaped Apollo, she eludes "Sol," her Bible.

Because of Lowell's inability to find a structure that will handle its parts,
the poem is the weakest in the volume. The logic is confused, and the plot
suffers from a noticeable repetition and lack of buildup. Some of the recollections are not pertinent and could be cut. Others remain vague and perplexing,
and the transitional devices are repetitious and mechanical. As the whole,
justified perhaps by the theme of the poem, is a presentation of the compulsive
repetitiousness of man, it offers little besides its gothic machinery to entice a
reader.

Despite these inadequacies, the poem's acceptance of Death resolves once
and for all on a worldly level the alternative of escape from the life-time cycle
posed in "Between the Porch and the Altar." The fact that Lowell offers a
worldly substitute in this volume is significant. It indicates, at least, that he
is no longer compelling all mankind to accept his view of contemplation as
the necessary and only means of regaining God's likeness. Sympathetically, he

seems to be reaching out to those whose lives may be best described as active and whose minds cannot comprehend the necessary abstraction of contemplation, people whose lives are contingent on events, and who, were they left without them, would have no lives. His reaching out to these people eliminates much from the wrenchings which filled his first volumes.

As the poem seeks no contemplative Truth or ecstasy, it completes the cycle of the religious direction in Lowell's work, the several sources of which include the contemplative tradition of St. Bernard and St. Bonaventure. The poet has abandoned one of these sources—religious contemplation—for the successful continuation of the others. This change, which some historians of drama designate "the exclusion of the deity from drama," is often termed by them the beginning of the real tragic vision, the point at which ritual becomes motivated human action.

From *The Poetic Themes of Robert Lowell* (Ann Arbor: Univ. of Michigan Press, 1965), pp. 74-87.

JOHN HOLLANDER

Robert Lowell's New Book

ROBERT LOWELL is probably the most distinguished American poet of his generation, and under any circumstances, the appearance of his first book in eight years would have to be a considerable event. For those readers who have not followed the periodical publication of a good many of the poems in *Life Studies* during the past few years, the event may be a rather surprising one as well. An abrupt change in subject and style appears at first glance to have taken place. The opening section of the book follows recognizable cadences (as at the end of *Beyond the Alps:* "Now Paris, our black classic, breaking up/like killer kings on an Etruscan cup") and casts itself in familiar forms (dramatic monologues, for example, of Marie de Medici and of *A Mad Negro Soldier Confined at Munich*) that are as characteristic of Mr. Lowell's previous work as is their excellence. But the remainder of the book (with the possible exception of two poems to Ford Madox Ford and George Santayana) will seem to represent an extremely sharp turning off an undeniably ascending straight path. This new course is made all the more startling, as well as all the more apparently divergent, perhaps, by reason of the currency, at the time of the book's publication, of a somewhat militant esthetic position equating strict prosody with a kind of literary repression—a poetic Reichian character armor, so to speak, and demanding a more "natural" national mode of poetic expression. For what seems most prominently to govern this new direction in Mr. Lowell's work is the association of a new autobiographical subject matter and a poetic form that has loosened almost unrecognizably in logic and meter.

I say *"seems* most prominently to govern" because I think that the continuities between these poems and the earlier ones are stronger, after all, than the divergences. The book's thematic structure is dominated by a pivotal, thirty-five page prose fragment of reminiscences, themselves somewhat fragmentary in nature, of the poet's family and of his native city. This prose section, entitled "91 Revere Street," glosses, and is in turn glossed by, the eleven poems that make up the first group of the section of the book called, after the title of the whole, "Life Studies." The final poems in this first group and those of the second concern the poet's recent life, rather than his childhood. The diction of all these poems varies considerably. In *Sailing Home from Rapallo,* for example, we find a vocabulary and a measure as hitherto well-known in Mr. Lowell's poetry as these:

The graveyard's soil was changing to stone—

so many of its deaths had been midwinter.
Dour and dark against the blinding snowdrifts,
its black brook and fir trunks were as smooth as masts.
A fence of spear-hafts
black-bordered its mostly Colonial grave-slates.

Despite the almost startling relaxation of the poet's accustomed iambic rhythm, the voice is utterly familiar here. On the other hand, something rather new appears when the tension of a whole, bare, almost prosaic passage of report will be packed into what is more image than figure, more glimpse, even, than image:

> All night the crib creaks;
> home from the healthy country to the sick city,
> my daughter in fever
> flounders in her chicken-colored sleeping bag.

These are the opening lines of *During Fever*. Again, at the end of what is almost the diary-entry and the easy ironies of the first paragraph of *Memories of West Street and Lepke*, we get much the same thing:

> I have a nine-months' daughter,
> young enough to be my granddaughter.
> Like the sun she rises in her flame-flamingo infants' wear.

The remainder of the poem, with its memories of the violence of imprisonment, is thus introduced with an image of passionate disruption of a kind that is ubiquitous in much of the poet's work (see the beginning of *Man and Wife*, for example: "Tamed by *Miltown*, we lie on Mother's bed;/the rising sun in war paint dyes us red").

   Then, too, there are passages of some length that seem to function as isolated fragments of intensely felt and even more intensely remembered experience, existing prior to, and underlying, the rather witty and polished paragraphs of *91 Revere Street*, with their predominantly scenic organization. The autobiographical poems of *Life Studies* are constructed around the glimpse, the remembered object, rather than, in a more novelistic way, around the scene, the event or the confrontation. In them a mere inventory often takes on a menacing air, a promise of either psychic violence or unimaginably deep comfort, even before some final, clinching image will strike the tone, finally committing the poem's attitude. Some lines from further on in *During Fever* exemplify this:

> Mother your master-bedroom
> looked away from the ocean.
> You had a window-seat,
> an electric blanket,
> a silver hot water bottle

> monogrammed like a hip-flask,
> Italian china fruity
> with bunches and berries
> and proper *putti*.
> Gold, yellow and green, the nuptial bed
> was as big as a bathroom.

From what I have quoted so far, it will be obvious that the poet has left behind him several of the schemes that typified the poems of *Lord Weary's Castle* by which he is best known. Tight stanza forms, melodramatically invoked Christian imagery, an almost rhetorical allusiveness now and then, all served to illuminate a Hell set not in contemporary Boston, but in a mythically powerful metamorphosis of that city into a half-actual, half-historical apparition—a metaphysical Boston yoking the felt present and the known past by violence together. But there has also existed another strain in Mr. Lowell's poetry that appears in several poems in *Lord Weary's Castle* and may be traced through the shorter poems in *The Mills of the Kavanaughs* (such as *Her Dead Brother, David and Bathsheba in the Public Garden* and, most particularly, *Thanksgiving's Over,* one of his finest poems altogether). It is this line that may be said to have reached fruition in the recent poems; its course may be followed from the section called "The Attic" from *The First Sunday in Lent,* or the opening of *Mary Winslow* ("Her Irish maids could never spoon out mush/Or orange juice enough") and other poems in the earlier book. The speaker is in most of these cases the protagonist of a dramatic monologue, as, for example, in *Between the Porch and the Altar:*

> It must have been a Friday. I could hear
> The top-floor typist's thunder and the beer
> That you had brought in cases hurt my head;
> I'd sent the pillows flying from my bed,
> I hugged my knees together and I gasped.

But the genre is the same even where the "I" of the poem seems to be more the poet himself, as in *The Death of the Sheriff:*

> The popping pine-cones flash
> Like shore-bait on his face in oils. My bile
> Rises, and beads of perspiration swell
> To flies and splash the *Parmachenie Belle*
> That I am scraping with my uncle's file.

It is true that, in both of these cases, it is the rigor of the rhymed pentameters and their unique energy that we associate with Mr. Lowell's work of this period. The attentive rigor of stanzas and often of couplets is generally absent from the newer poems. But this is not to say by any means that metrical control and power have been abandoned here. A characteristic quality of Mr. Lowell's pentameter lines has always been one of lumped tension, of a half-awkward clotting-up of the otherwise strict alternation of weak and strong syllables with consonantal clusters that seem always on the verge of dominating the rhythm. The grotesque opening lines of the poem to Ford Madox Ford in the present book seem almost self-parody in their overuse of this phenomenon: "The lobbed ball plops, then dribbles to the cup . . . /(a birdie, Fordie)." This sort of texture is used far more successfully however, when the commanding pentameter movement is no longer there to "save" it. The conclusion of *Waking in the Blue* starts off with just such a jerky, fretful music:

> . . . Cock of the walk,
> I strut in my turtle-necked French sailor's jersey
> before the metal shaving mirrors,
> and see the shaky future grow familiar
> in the pinched, indigenous faces
> of these thoroughbred mental cases,
> twice my age and half my weight.
> We are all old-timers,
> each of us holds a locked razor.

The control exercised by the syntactical line-breaks, by the occasional half and full rhymes, and by the pulsations, of metrical tension between more strictly and more loosely related lines is very much like, *mutatis mutandis,* the kind of control exercised by the tighter prosody of the earlier poems. It is merely that the material is less violent and less likely itself to get out of hand, seeming to require less in the way of restraining devices, metrical, metaphorical or mythical. Often when writing of his baby daughter, Mr. Lowell moves into an apocalyptic mode through the use of a glimpse of color, as in the passages quoted earlier, or in *Home After Three Months Away:*

> Though I am forty-one,
> not forty now, the time I put away
> was child's-play. After thirteen weeks
> my child still dabs her cheeks
> to start me shaving. When
> we dress her in her sky-blue corduroy,
> she changes to a boy,
> and floats my shaving brush
> and washcloth in the flush. . . .
> Dearest, I cannot loiter here
> in lather like a polar bear.

Only after the shock of "sky-blue" has expended itself, does the poem move into the wry mode. Here as elsewhere in *Life Studies,* however, the imagery unites not the actual and the imagined, but rather the worlds of child and adult, the realms of the variously remembered, near and distant. The over-arching cosmos that contains all of these, seeing them simultaneously, is the world of these poems. In considering the interior of that world, I remember Delmore Schwartz's line: "How all things flash! how all things flare!" But the light on the objects and people in these poems is generated with less heat than is that of the refining fire of the previous books. In *Where the Rainbow Ends,* Mr. Lowell concluded *Lord Weary's Castle* by asking almost of his own poetic imagination

> . . . What can the dove of Jesus give
> You now but wisdom, exile? Stand and live,
> The dove has brought an olive branch to eat.

The question remained for some time exactly what sort of wisdom it was toward which the poet was to move in his subsequent work. In the title poem of *The Mills of the Kavanaughs* he made what was perhaps a last, not completely successful attempt to criticize in a state of near-prophetic terror a world that he had himself created; his theme was still "History" (as he rang a surprisingly fundamental change on T. S. Eliot's line) "is now and New England." In the present book, the olive branch symbolic of both peace and of sustenance after the deluge appears only in the facts of life and the things of this world, in the bountiful harvest of the "Fallings from us," the "vanishings" into whose nature the Imagination must needs direct its most unrelenting researches. *Life Studies* is withal a much less spectacular book than its two predecessors, but it is unbelievably moving.

From *Poetry,* 95 (Oct. 1959), 41-46.

M. L. ROSENTHAL

Poetry as Confession

LIFE STUDIES. By Robert Lowell. Farrar, Straus & Cudahy. 90 pp. $3.50.

EMILY DICKINSON once called publication "the auction of the mind." Robert Lowell seems to regard it more as soul's therapy. The use of poetry for the most naked kind of confession grows apace in our day. We are now far from the great Romantics who, it is true, spoke directly of their emotions but did not give the game away even to themselves. They found, instead, cosmic equations and symbols, transcendental reconciliations with "this lime-tree bower my prison," titanic melancholia in the course of which, merging his sense of tragic fatality with the evocations of the nightingale's song, the poet lost his personal complaint in the music of universal forlornness. Later, Whitman took American poetry to the very edge of the confessional in his *Calamus* poems and in the quivering avowal of his helplessness before the seductions of "blind loving wrestling touch, sheath'd hooded sharp-tooth'd touch." More recently, under the influence of the Symbolists, Eliot and Pound brought us into the forbidden realm itself, yet even in their work a certain indirection masks the poet's actual face and psyche from greedy eyes.

Lowell removes the mask. His speaker is unequivocally himself, and it is hard not to think of *Life Studies* as a series of personal confidences, rather shameful, that one is honor-bound not to reveal. About half the book, the prose section called "91 Revere Street," is essentially a public discrediting of his father's manliness and character, as well as of the family and social milieu of his childhood. Another section, the concluding sequence of poems grouped under the heading "Life Studies," reinforces and even repeats these motifs, bringing them to bear on the poet's psychological problems as an adult. The father, Naval officer *manqué* and then businessman and speculator *manqué*, becomes a humiliating symbol of the failure of a class and of a kind of personality. Lowell's contempt for him is at last mitigated by adult compassion, though I wonder if a man can allow himself this kind of ghoulish operation on his father without doing his own spirit incalculable damage. But the damage has clearly been in the making a long time, and Lowell knows very well that he is doing violence to himself most of all:

> . . . I hear
> my ill-spirit sob in each blood cell,
> as if my hand were at its throat. . . .

He does not spare himself in these poems, at least two of which have to do with sojourns in mental hospitals and his return home from them. We have grotesque glimpses into his marital life. "Man and Wife," for instance, begins: "Tamed by *Miltown,* we lie on Mother's bed." It later tells how

> All night I've held your hand,
> as if you had
> a fourth time faced the kingdom of the mad—
> its hackneyed speech, its homicidal eye—
> and dragged me home alive. . . .

"My mind's not right," says the speaker in "Skunk Hour," the poem which ends the book. It is partly Lowell's apology for what he has been saying in these pieces, like Gerontion's mumbling that he is only "an old man, a dull head among windy spaces." And it is partly his assertion that he cannot breathe without these confessions, however rank they may be, and that the things he has been talking about are too stubbornly alive to be ignored:

> I stand on top
> of our back steps and breathe the rich air—
> a mother skunk with her column of kittens swills the garbage pail.
> She jabs her wedge-head in a cup
> of sour cream, drops her ostrich tail,
> and will not scare.

It will be clear that my first impression while reading *Life Studies* was that it is impure art, magnificently stated but unpleasantly egocentric—somehow resembling the triumph of the skunks over the garbage cans. Since its self-therapeutic motive is so obvious and persistent, something of this impression sticks all the way. But as the whole work floods into view the balance shifts decisively. Lowell is still the wonderful poet of "The Quaker Graveyard in Nantucket," the poet of power and passion whose driving aesthetic of anguish belies the "frizzled, stale and small" condition he attributes to himself. He may be wrong in believing that what has happened to New England's elite is necessarily an embodiment of the state of American culture, the whole maggoty character of which he feels he carries about in his own person. But he is not wrong in looking at the culture through the window of psychological break- down. Too many other American poets, no matter what their social class and family history, have reached the same point in recent years. Lowell is foremost among them in the energy of his uncompromising honesty.

Furthermore, *Life Studies* is not merely a collection of small moment-by- moment victories over hysteria and self-concealment. It is also a beautifully articulated poetic sequence. I say "articulated," but the impact of the sequence is of four intensifying waves of movement that smash at the reader's feelings and break repeatedly over his mind. The poems that make up the opening movement are not personal in the sense of the rest of the book. They are poems of violent contradiction, a historical overture to define the disintegration of a world. In the first a train journeys from Rome to Paris at mid-century. The "querulous hush-hush" of its wheels passes over the Alps and beyond them, but nowhere in the altitudes to which it rises does it touch the sanely brilliant heights of ancient myth and thought. For its riders there are, at one terminal, the hysteria of *bella Roma,* where "the crowds at San Pietro screamed *Papa*" at the pronouncement of the dogma of Mary's assumption and where "the Duce's lynched, bare, booted skull still spoke"; and at the other terminal, the self-destructive freedom of "Paris, our black classic." The next poem reaches far enough back in time to reveal the welter of grossly sensual, mindlessly grasping egotism that attended the birth of the modern age. Marie de Medici, "the banker's daughter," soliloquizes about "blood and pastime," the struggle between monarchy and the "pilfering, pillaging democracies," the assassination of her husband. The third poem returns from modern Europe and its bloody beginnings to our own American moment. All that turbulence of recent centuries now seems frozen into intellectual and moral death:

> Ice, ice. Our wheels no longer move.
> Look, the fixed stars, all just alike
> as lack-land atoms, split apart,
> and the Republic summons Ike,
> the mausoleum in her heart.

But then the fourth poem hurls at us the monologue of a mad Negro soldier confined at Munich. Here the wit, the audacious intimacy, the acutely bizarre tragic sense of Lowell's language take on jet-speed. In this monologue the breakdown of traditional meanings and cultural distinctions is dramatized in the frenzy of one contemporary figure. Thus Lowell begins to zero in on his main target, himself as the damned speaking-sensibility of his world. The humiliated, homicidal fury of the Negro soldier throws its premonitory shadow over the disturbed "comedy" of "91 Revere Street" which follows. It helps us to see, beneath the "Jamesian" nuances of relationship in a society of ritual pretensions but no center of gravity, how anguished is this prose section's murderous dissection of the poet's parents and its complaint against a childhood gone awry. In this way it prepares us for the personal horrors with which the book closes.

But before that long, devastating final wave of poems, there is a smaller one, corresponding in gathering force with the first group. This third wave is again made up of four poems, each of them about a modern writer with whom Lowell feels kinship as an embattled and alienated spirit. Following hard upon the prose, these poems clearly say: "This is what the predatory centuries, and the soul-devouring world in which I walked the maze of my childhood, have done to man's creativity." Lowell first portrays Ford Madox Ford, the "mammoth mumbler" cheated out of his earned rewards, standing up to Lloyd George and, later, scratching along in America, sick and "gagged for air." Then, dear to Lowell's heart, the self-exiled Santayana looms before us—"free-thinking Cath-

74 M. L. ROSENTHAL

olic infidel." The third poem recreates with sentimental bitterness a winter
Lowell and Delmore Schwartz spent at Harvard in 1946. Nothing could be
more pathetically open about Lowell's state of mind concerning himself and
his art than the parts of their conversation he chooses to record and even to
italicize:

> . . . "Let Joyce and Freud,
> the Masters of Joy,
> be our guests here," you said. The room was filled
> with cigarette smoke circling the paranoid,
> inert gaze of Coleridge, back
> from Malta—his eyes lost in flesh, lips baked and black. . . .
> You said:
> *"We poets in our youth begin in sadness;*
> *thereof in the end come despondency and madness;*
> Stalin has had two cerebral hemorrhages!"

The ironic facetiousness that so often marks Schwartz's writing and conversation is here absorbed by Lowell into a vision of unrelieved breakdown
centered on the image of Coleridge's "paranoid gaze" in the picture. That
image, together with the mocking allusion to Stalin as one of "we poets" who
come at last to madness, brings past and present, and all political and psychological realities, into a single focus of defeat. Then in the fourth poem, "Words
for Hart Crane," the group comes to a climax paralleling that of "A Mad Negro
Soldier" in the first group. Crane's brief, self-destructive career is seen as the
demand of the creative spirit, deliberately wearing the most loathsome mask
it can find, for unquestioning love from the culture that he has rejected it. Here,
just before he plunges back into his major theme, the "life studies" of himself
and his family, Lowell again—at the most savagely committed pitch he can
command—presents the monologue of a dramatically suffering figure whose
predicament has crucial bearing on his own.

In large part, the fourteen poems of the final section echo the prose of "91
Revere Street." But they echo it as a storm echoes the foreboding sultriness
of a threatening spell of weather before it. Apart from the obvious differences
that verse makes, they break out of the cocoon of childhood-mentality that
somehow envelops "91 Revere Street" despite its more sophisticated aspects.
Lowell, like Yeats and Thomas, casts over his autobiographical prose a certain
whimsy (though often morbid) and childlike half-awareness. But the poems are
overborne by sadness first and then by the crash of disaster. Side by side Lowell
places memories of his confinement in mental hospitals and a denigration of
his great act of defiance as a conscientious objector in World War II which
led to his imprisonment for a year:

> I was a fire-breathing Catholic C.O.,
> and made my manic statement,
> telling off the state and president. . . .

The only poem of this group in which he does not talk in his own person, " 'To Speak of Woe That Is in Marriage,' " is a monologue by the wife of a lecherous, "hopped-up" drunkard. It is placed strategically just before the last poem, "Skunk Hour," and after "Man and Wife," in which Lowell makes certain we know he is discussing his own marriage, and it is a deliberate plunge into the depths of the theme of degradation at all but the last moment. Finally, "Skunk Hour," full of indirections and nuances that bring the sickness of our world as a whole back into the scene to restore a more universal vision, reaches a climax of self-contempt and of pure symbol-making. This is Lowell's fantastic, terrifying skunk-image for the secret self's inescapable drive to assure itself of continued life—

> I myself am hell;
> nobody's here—
>
> only skunks, that search
> in the moonlight for a bite to eat.
> They march on their soles up Main Street:
> white stripes, moonstruck eyes' red fire
> under the chalk-dry and spar spire
> of the Trinitarian Church.

Life Studies brings to culmination one line of development in our poetry of the utmost importance. Technically, it is an experiment in the form of the poetic sequence comparable to *Mauberley* and *The Bridge*. To build a great poem out of the predicament and horror of the lost Self has been the recurrent effort of the most ambitious poetry of the last century. It is too early to say whether *Life Studies* is great art. Enough, for the moment, to realize that it is inescapably encompassing art.

From *The Nation,* 19 Sept. 1959, pp. 154-55.

DESALES STANDERWICK

Pieces too Personal

THIS SMALL volume, the first to issue from Robert Lowell in a long while, does not, in my opinion, match his remarkable achievement in either *Lord Weary's Castle* or *The Mills of the Cavanaughs*. This observation is strengthened by the presence in the book of a particularly well-written memoir entitled "91 Revere Street" that comes through to the reader with greater sharpness, clarity and spirit than many of the poems.

Part of the disappointment in the volume stems from the subject-matter of the poems. The majority of the poems are personal reflections on the poet's life—his childhood, grandparents, places associated with his life, his mother, his own illness and marriage and fatherhood. But so excellent is the writing in the prose memoir that these poems do not shine out with the same happy and careful expression of his observations. The universality of the experiences of human life, the piercing judgments on a deceptive way of living, the almost prophet-like vision of a gigantic mind—all present in the former volumes—do not appear in these poems that take for their starting points either very particular childhood memories or admired authors (Ford Madox Ford, George Santayana, Delmore Schwartz, Hart Crane), or individualized personifications ("The Mad Negro Soldier," "The Banker's Daughter," "To Speak of the Woe That Is in Marriage"). Somehow the author does not seem to get beyond the limited vision that enwraps the subject-matter of the various poems and to see the universal truth that might be present in the individual instance.

Lowell, of course, has his own idiom, and it is his manner of expression that made his former poems jump off the pages and dazzle the reader's eyes, the more so in that his use of rhyme was so expert, so exact, and most often unobtrusive. The memoir-poems in this volume are unrhymed; about five other poems have rhymes scattered through them; only seven are fully and somewhat intricately and artistically rhymed. His use of rhyme was an important quality of Lowell's poetry since it gave part of the beauty and music and unity to many of his former poems.

The same observation can be made about the imagery of the poems in the present collection. Formerly, the imagery was rich, exuberant, unique, yet always functional and more than likely tightly unified, giving the poems that rare quality of true vision granted the poet, and shared with the world around him.

The "family" poems in *Life Studies* lack this imagery save in rare instances: " . . . its alley of poplars/paraded from Grandmother's rose garden/to a scarey stand of virgin pine . . . "; "Distorting drops of water/pinpricked my face in the basin's mirror"; " . . . the clump of virgin pine still stretched patchy ostrich necks/over the disused millpond's fragrantly woodstained water . . . "; "his thermos of shockless coffee . . . "; the captured newts lay dumb "as scrolls of candied grapefruit peel."

What these lines profess is a keen memory and a sharp eye for detail, being profuse in descriptions of houses, rooms, bric-a-brac, dress, stances and poses. Many of these descriptions are happily worded; it may be that these poems derive their universality in the accurate and quite honest portraitures they give of human beings—although, again, in their details and in their overall aspects, they could be more closely knit together and unified. I will take just a few of the poems for special comment.

The short poem, "For Sale," is a brief picture-poem in which the poet states that his father's cottage, possessed for only a year, had to be sold when the father died. His mother lingered in the house the day they were to leave. The cottage was a "sheepish" plaything; the furniture, out of place in the country, seemed to be waiting nervously for the moving men. His mother had the stupefied, dull look of a person who had failed to debark at the correct train station. The poet sympathizes with the cottage as if it had received a bad deal. His tone implies he condemns, not too seriously, the lavish wilfulness with which it has been outfitted. But what effects him most is the sight of his mother sitting abstractedly near a window, realizing that the disposal of the cottage is one more concrete evidence of her husband's death and absence. One is tempted almost to let his eyes skip from the title "For Sale" down to his words about his mother, as if he were making some mental connection between the two.

The poem, "For George Santayana," sympathetic in tone and outlook, seems to be the result of a personal visit to the Catholic monastery where George Santayana spent the last years of his life. It opens with a description of what has now become the typical European viewpoint of Americans as "souvenir-deranged" until it speaks directly to Santayana, calling him that "stray spirit, who'd found/the Church too good to be believed," although "the world too prosaic to be lived in" might more accurately describe the straying, aloof attitude of Santayana.

As in so many of his poems, Lowell continues here that bridging of history that establishes his ideas and moods with the tradition that has gone before. The Roman and Greek worlds creep in with the references to the Circus and the Mithraic Temple, lying as they do on his way to Santo Stefano, representing the Christian Rome; in any event, Roman or Christian, old or modern, it is to him "Bella Roma," as he avers in the poem, "Beyond the Alps." The world of philosophical thought, so dear to Santayana though he appears to have been so individualistic in his approach and development, is present in the references to Socrates and Alcibiades.

The poems in this volume are not heavily laden with the imagery that we usually associate with the sensitive and fanciful mind of a poet. This to me is a weakness in the writing, especially in the remembrance poems. In the

Santayana poem, the conclusion does contain this magic of imagery, and presents a fine word-picture of the aged philosopher:

> near ninety,
> still unbelieving, unconfessed and unreceived,
> true to your boyish shyness of the Bride.
> Old trooper, I see your child's red crayon pass,
> bleeding deletions on the galleys you hold
> under your throbbing magnifying glass,
> that worn arena, where the whirling sand
> and broken-hearted lions lick your hand
> refined by bile as yellow as a lump of gold.

There are in this collection six sonnets, if we include the three that loosely make up the poem, "Beyond the Alps." The three single sonnets differ in subject-matter (marriage, Hart Crane, Inauguration Day) as well as in rhyme scheme and meter. In this former poetry Lowell used the two-line rhyme in as masterful a fashion as possible. In this volume he has abandoned it save in occasional places, as in the sonnet, "To Speak of Woe That Is in Marriage." Also in his earlier work, Lowell was almost scrupulous in his use of a quasi-poetic diction. Now he resorts to expressions like "dope or screw" (as nouns), "hopped up husband," "screwball" and "Mayflower screwballs." True, in context these are from monologues spoken by types or particular people; still, his imagination used to be able to come up with words more exact and more poetic.

The sonnet, "Words for Hart Crane," puts into the mouth of Crane harsh words the tragic poet might speak to some "stranger in America." The poem is earthy and hard, using slang prose like "phoney gold-plated laurels" and "wolfing the stray lambs." It catches the literary ranking of Crane by references to Whitman (who had great influence on Crane), to Catullus, and to Shelley. The fourteen lines are as succinct and accurate a biography of this misguided genius as could be found, although omitting any mention of Crane's alcoholism. The problem of a man's free will might possibly be seen in, "I . . . used to play my role/of homosexual," as if a human being, plagued by perverse and not so latent desires, had to become their slave; as though that were the role assigned to him in life and he had no choice but to play it. The last two lines preserve the poem from becoming too strident and harsh an indictment of American literature's neglect of Crane, whose work gains greater stature as the years pass.

Life Studies also contains a thirty-five page memoir of Lowell's earlier life, memories that "hover . . . in recollection," where "The things and their owners come back urgent with life and meaning." Somehow, there is little of Robert Lowell or his doings in these memoirs; rather, they are a small boy's reflections, gathered and matured in retrospect, upon his "forlornly fatherless" father, and his haughty and chilly mother; upon his home at 91 Revere Street, which acts as the focal point for his launching out into the world of education; upon the Sunday dinners and visitors, naval and otherwise, at Revere Street; upon the "rocklike" things—Major Mordecai Myers' portrait in the forefront—connected with the house and fastened securely in his memory. It is the type of rambling, loose memoir that I personally feel every adult should write for himself so that he might preserve and clarify those conscious impressions of what his childhood and home life were.

Not everyone's prose would have the pungency and kick and open honesty of Lowell's writing. Nor would they be so blessed as to be surrounded by phrase-makers and quotable talkers. Lowell's mother is by far the best. She spoke of the family receiving some trust-fund money "not grand enough to corrupt us but sufficient to prevent Daddy from being entirely at the mercy of his salary." Other memorable comments include: "We are barely perched on the outer rim of the hub of decency"; "Alone and at night an amateur driver is unsafe in a car"; "Your inebriated sailors have littered my doorstep with the dregs of Scollay Square"; "I have always believed carving [of dinner roasts] to be *the* gentlemanly talent." Captain Atkinson was in her displeasure because he was "unable to tell one woman from another." The whole of this essay is delightful, truthful (we presume), warm-hearted and memorable.

If I have been too harsh in my judgment on these latest Lowell poems, it is because my disappointment arises from a comparison of those works with his former poems. There are, be it known, many excellent passages in the poems—incisive phrases, clear pictures, a diction for the most part unique, yet spontaneous. The stamp of an original writer is upon these lines. The difficulty, I think, comes from the subject-matter, which is often extremely personal, sometimes embarrassing, and occasionally too unique to be universalized.

From *Renascence*, 13 (1960), 53-56.

GEOFFREY HILL

Robert Lowell: "Contrasts and Repetitions"

Robert Lowell: The First Twenty Years. By Hugh B. Staples. Faber.
Imitations. By Robert Lowell. Faber.

IN THE final chapter of Hugh B. Staple's *Robert Lowell: The First Twenty Years* the poet is quoted as saying:

'When I finished *Life Studies*, I was left hanging on a question mark. I am still hanging there. I don't know whether it is a death-rope or a lifeline.'

It would be dangerously easy for a reviewer, taking his cue from Lowell's tone, to decide that the recent book, *Imitations,* is uncertain interim-work; a series of snatches at the lifeline or a toying with the death-rope. This hypothesis shrivels in the light of such beautifully-finished artefacts. Alternatively, on the basis of evidence supplied by Mr. Staples, one might be equally tempted to claim these 'versions and free translations' as the proper consummation of the first twenty years. It seems demonstrable that 'imitation' has been, from the start, one of Lowell's most resolute and fruitful methods. In an interview printed in *The Paris Review* (no. 25), he recalls that his first book, *Land of Unlikeness* (1944), included 'several paraphrases of early Christian poems'. *Lord Weary's Castle* (1946) contained the celebrated 'The Ghost (after Sextus Propertius)' together with 'War (after Rimbaud)' and others. And even in *Life Studies* (1959), which marks an emphatic change of direction in Lowell's style, the precedent still, tenuously, holds. The poem 'To speak of Woe That Is in Marriage':

'started as a translation of Catullus. I don't know what traces are left, but it couldn't have been written without the Catullus.' (*Paris Review*)

It is also noteworthy that the name *Imitations* seems to hark back to the author's note in *Poems* 1938-49 (1950):

'When I use the *after* below the title of a poem, what follows is not a translation but an imitation.'

The connotations of the word, however, are fluid. Lowell now (1962) speaks of 'poetic translation—I would call it an imitation', thus presenting the two key-terms in alignment rather than in opposition. Even so, the methods employed in *Imitations* where:

'I have dropped lines, moved lines, moved stanzas, changed images and altered metre and intent'

are consistent with those employed throughout Lowell's poetic career.

One of the most rewarding sections of Mr. Staple's valuable study is that part of the Appendix in which he sets out the sources, references and analogues for some of Lowell's most celebrated passages. Here, for example, is the opening of 'The Quaker Graveyard in Nantucket':

> A brackish reach of shoal off Madaket,—
> The sea was still breaking violently and night
> Had steamed into our North Atlantic Fleet,
> When the drowned sailor clutched the drag-net. Light
> Flashed from his matted head and marble feet,
> He grappled at the net
> With the coiled, hurdling muscles of his thighs:
> The corpse was bloodless, a botch of reds and whites,
> Its open, staring eyes
> Were lustreless dead-lights
> Or cabin-windows on a stranded hulk
> Heavy with sand.

And here is the passage from Thoreau's *Cape Cod* which inspired it:

' . . . it was now Tuesday morning, and the sea was still breaking violently on the rocks . . . I saw many marble feet and matted heads . . . and one livid, swollen, and mangled body of a drowned girl . . . the coiled-up wreck of a human hulk, gashed by the rocks or fishes, so that the bone and muscle were exposed, but quite bloodless,— merely red and white,—with wide-open and staring eyes, yet lustreless, dead-lights; or like the cabin windows of a stranded vessel, filled with sand. . . . '

The indebtedness is obvious, but equally apparent is the imaginative kindling, the pungent life of Lowell's own metaphors:

'night/Had steamed into our North Atlantic Fleet'

is both prosaic and sinister, a communiqué formalizing the final helplessness of man, and anticipating the loudly futile 'salute' at the end of the first section. Lowell also contrives the sheen of All-American athleticism, of posturing virility, in the dead man's involuntary movements. His appearance is a travesty of gymnastic buoyancy:

'He grappled at the net
With the coiled, hurdling muscles of his thighs . . . '

And Lowell, adding 'botch' to Thoreau's 'red and white' ensures that the energy
here is grim in its remoteness from human contact, like the energy of a
rawly-painted activated dummy.

In such a passage, the original grief for Warren Winslow, dead at Sea, the
objective pity assimilated from Thoreau, are redefined by a fine management
of technique. The writing is deeply-felt and strongly-mannered: the feeling is
embodied in the mannerism. Occasionally Staples reveals a transient uneasiness
with such requisites as 'making'. Of an early Lowell poem, 'On the Eve of the
Feast of the Immaculate Conception, 1942', he says:

'The language here reflects in part a young poet's conscious striving for
novelty; it is barely rescued from bathos by the dignity and strength of the
religious emotion that produced it. In these poems, the quasi-facetious
manner is usually balanced by the sincerity of the poet's faith.'

One might have little difficulty in accepting Staple's criticism of such poems
if his objections were couched in somewhat different terms. But it is necessary
to dispute his premises as they stand. One would argue that the poem has
yet to be written that could be rescued from 'bathos' by the 'dignity and
strength' or the 'sincerity' of any emotion. If a poem does preserve itself from
unintentional bathos it is not by virtue of an extraneous, or even a fundamental,
emotion, but by the validity of its achieved statements: by their propriety or
by their timed and weighed—their 'quasi-facetious'—impropriety. Lowell himself has said, in the *Paris Review* interview:

'I think it [the poem] can only have integrity apart from the beliefs; that
no political position, religious position, position of generosity, or what have
you, can make a poem good. It's all to the good if a poem *can* use politics,
or theology, or gardening, or anything that has its own validity aside from
poetry. But these things will never *per se* make a poem.'

'Theology, or gardening . . . ': here, of course, the poet can afford to appear
more relaxed than the critic. And granted, in Lowell's case, a poetry persistent
in its manipulation of religious metaphor, Mr. Staples is justified in worrying
about the implications of such work. One is more inclined to take issue with
certain of his actual pronouncements than to quibble about his basic concern.
When he says, for example,

'In several of the poems the religious obsessions reassert their dark majesty
. . . '

he seems to be suggesting, if not requiring, for religious involvement *per se* the kind of potency that Lowell himself is willing to disclaim. A suggestion, rather less ambiguous than Staple's, might be that dramatized situations of religious obsession are prominent in Lowell's work. One would still be free to determine whether these really do project a 'dark majesty' or whether one simply desires that they should.

The rich European and American legacies of revelation and self-revelation may be said to focus for Lowell on the life and work of Jonathan Edwards, whose biography he once planned to write (and which, in a sense, he *has* written in an abbreviated and lyric form!). In 'Mr. Edwards and the Spider' where, as Staples points out, 'nearly every line . . . contains phraseology taken directly from the writings of the noted eighteenth-century Calvinist', Lowell employs a technique which affects the overt scrupulousness and soul-tightening with suggestions of megalomania and hysteria:

> 'How long would it seem burning! Let there pass
> A minute, ten, ten trillion; but the blaze
> Is infinite, eternal:'

Here, formal commination jerks to-and-fro in the hyperbole of a fearfully-boasting child. Whether Lowell got this from Edwards, or made it up in the style of Edwards, hardly matters. What does matter is the imaginative disposition of the material, which releases both the tone of magisterial dogmatism and the note of childish exaggeration and causes them to interact.

Although Mr. Staples deserves our gratitude for a thorough and sensitive study of the way in which influence becomes utterance in Lowell's poetry, he seems occasionally less happy with the formal position of the poet as rhetorician than with the human enigma of the poet as troubled believer. Of the apostrophe to Grant in the poem 'Inauguration Day: January 1953' ('Horseman, your sword is in the groove!') Staples says:

> 'The net effect of this is to lessen the impact of the poem; it becomes a lampoon instead of a satire because there is a question in the reader's mind as to Lowell's real convictions.'

A sense of uneasiness as to the effective range of the slangy 'in the groove' is justifiable. Even so, Staple's employment of 'because' seems logically suspect. It is hard to accept the idea of a casual repercussion from a reader's bewilderment to a poem's real nature, which is the proper concern of the poet's imaginative tact. And since Lowell chose to conclude this particular poem:

> 'and the Republic summons Ike,
> the mausoleum in her heart.'

—Staples might have risked the suggestion that Lowell *meant* to write a lampoon.

The question of intention, as one would expect, arises with some frequency in a reading of *Imitations*. It is open to suggestion that Lowell, in parts of the book, is at least aware of the possibilities of the lampoonist's art. His thick strokes are coolly and self-consciously applied. In 'The Swan', Baudelaire's

> 'Je pense à la négresse, amaigrie et phthisique,
> Piétinant dans la boue, et cherchant, l'oeil hagard . . . '

becomes:

> 'I think of you, tubercular and sick,
> blindly stamping through puddles, Jeanne Duval . . . '

—a deliberate coarsening of the original effect. It is as though we are intended to recognize, in Lowell's poem, that the lyric maintains a perilous autonomy against mundane attrition. It shows itself scarred at the edge, somewhat distorted, as though from a partial melting-down.

In Lowell's rendering of Leopardi's 'A Silvia', the imitation is made to exacerbate the original. Where Leopardi says (I give Mr. George Kay's *Penguin* translation):

> 'Sometimes leaving my pleasant studies and the soiled pages where my first years and the best part of myself were spent. . . . '

Lowell develops the suggestion:

> 'I could forget
> the fascinating studies in my bolted room,
> where my life was burning out,
> and the heat
> of my writings made the letters wriggle and melt
> under drops of sweat.'

Lowell creates for Leopardi a passage of self-revelation in which he is made to expose a more febrile state-of-mind than he originally intended. The terrors of Leopardi's life are made to obtrude, in an exaggerated way, upon the plain statements of the poem, so that where he originally wrote 'your mortal life' he now says:

> 'this life overhung by death'

and his 'fascinating studies' in the 'bolted room' are suggestive of onanistic excitement.

One would accept this as a possible view of a life so spiritually and physically desolate as Leopardi's; and as a restatement of the romantic hypothesis that poetry is a substitute for the poet's personal deficiencies. Less imaginatively justifiable, perhaps, is Lowell's contribution to Baudelaire's 'Un Voyage à Cythère'. In the original tenth stanza, lines 3 and 4 read:

> 'Une plus grande bête au milieu s'agitait
> Comme un exécuteur entouré de ses aides.'

Lowell has:

> 'a huge antediluvian reptile muscled
> through them like an executioner with his aides.'

This seems to be exploiting, not so much an instinctive revulsion, as a gamut of ostentatiously Freudian suggestion.

Although any interference with original effect, and any introduction of innuendo, is theoretically permissible in the kind of work that Lowell is attempting, there are occasions when psychological or aesthetic relevance is replaced by a kind of fashionable window-display. Take the closing stanzas of 'The Swan':

> 'I think of people who have lost the luck
> they never find again, and waste their powers,
> like wolf-nurses giving grief a tit to suck,
> or public orphans drying up like flowers;
>
> and in this forest, on my downward drag,
> my old sorrow lets out its lion's roar.
> I think of Paris raising the white flag,
> drowned sailors, fallen girls . . . and many more!'

There is, perhaps, a too-fashionable toughness in the use here of 'tit' and 'drag'. In the imitation of Rimbaud's 'Au Cabaret-Vert' the word 'tit' is appropriate to that poem's situation and tone. In 'The Swan' it is not, and Lowell's insistence on using it seems a linguistic and poetic insensitivity. Mr. Francis Scarfe translates the original as:

> 'and suck the breast of Sorrow like a good mother-wolf'

which isn't terribly modern, but may be justified by Scarfe's note on the proper rhetoric of this poem:

> ' . . . the sublime compassion of the aria in the

second part, followed by the absolute fall into
prose , ending on a single note, on a kind of
"etcetera" in the "bien d'autres encore!"'
Baudelaire: The Penguin Poets: p. xlii)

Lowell retains the original sense at the end—'and many more!'—but his
resolute use of vulgarisms in the proceding lines means that the vital sense of
contrast is dissipated and that the marvellous prosaic power of the final few
words is lost. It is true that the implications of Lowell's

'like wolf-nurses giving grief a tit to suck'

may be rather different from those of:

'Et tettent la Douleur comme une bonne louve!'

—in Lowell's poem the 'wolf-nurses' might be whores—but it is still arguable
that, in retaining the Baudelairean ending, Lowell has committed himself to
the problem of achieving the 'absolute fall into prose' and that he has not
succeeded in this.

There are splendid things throughout the book. 'Sic Transit'—imitated from
Hebel's 'Die Vergänglichkeit' and 'The Landlord'—imitated from Pasternak—
are impressive; and there are instances of fine intuition, as when the line:

'Et leur versait parfois quelque sale caresse'

from Baudelaire's 'La Beatrice' is rendered:

'and sometimes tossing them a *stale* caress.'

—which, in the context, seems very just and powerful.

The imitation of 'Un Voyage à Cythère' provides an instance of what might
be termed 'cosmic redeployment':

'Les yeux étaient deux trous, et du ventre effondré,
Les intestins pesants lui coulaient sur les cuisses,
Et ses bourreaux, gorgés de hideuses délices,
L'avaient à coups de bec absolument châtré.'

'His eyes were holes and his important paunch
oozed lazy, looping innards down his hips;
those scavengers, licking sweetmeats from their lips,
had hung his pouch and penis on a branch.'

Lowell substitutes for 'effondré' ('broken-open', 'gutted') the word 'important' which is, perhaps, a take-over from 'intestins pesants' in the following line, since 'pesant' has metaphysical, as well as physical, connotations. 'Important paunch', then, becomes such a travesty of dignity that the birds' beaks might be called puncturing instruments in a double sense. In Lowell's fourth line:

> 'had hung his pouch and penis on a branch'

the farcical alternative 'his bowler-hat and umbrella' is not unthinkable. If this is ludicrous, it could be said that Baudelaire created the precedent by calling his victim 'ridicule pendu'. Even so, Lowell's sequence of grim buffoonery turns the hanged man into a figure of aldermanic caricature, closer perhaps to the essence of 'l'esprit Belge' than Baudelaire might have wished. And this emphasis must distort the meaning of that cry of recognition, self-identification, and self-scourged narcissism, with which both Baudelaire and Lowell end the poem.

These problems demand attention because Lowell, in his introduction to *Imitations,* has stressed the importance of 'tone' and has cited Pasternak's dictum that, in poetry, 'tone is of course everything'. Lowell says:

> 'I have been reckless with literal meaning, and laboured hard to get the tone.'

He continues:

> 'I have tried to write live English and to do what my authors might have done if they were writing their poems now and in America.'

It is possible that between these two statements a shift in intention has taken place, and that the method has moved from one of 'getting the tone' to one of dramatization. This is wholly valid, provided that the imitator knows precisely at what point he is becoming a dramatist.

An illustration of this last point may be obtained from Lowell's version of Baudelaire's 'Le Gouffre'. Lowell's contribution:

> 'I cuddle the insensible blank air'

seems to glance towards the famous entry in Baudelaire's Journal:

> 'I have cultivated my hysteria with delight and terror . . . '

so that 'cuddle' is both dramatization and critique of 'delight'. In its way, Lowell's line is splendid, though it takes self-revelation to a point from which it is as difficult to draw back as to go on. The decisive note of self-parody having been struck, its harmonics can be detected throughout the poem. Where Baudelaire, in the final line, originally wrote:

> '—Ah! ne jamais sortir des Nombres et des Etres!'

Lowell has:

> 'Ah never to escape from numbers and form!'

In the selection of 'form' to replace 'Beings' there is a touchiness that typifies the poem. Baudelaire's 'Le Gouffre' is a sonnet. Lowell imitates it in *thirteen* lines, which is a nice irregularity, a titillation of disorder. Much of the skill and appeal of a poem such as this rests in the fact that it can enjoy the ultimate in selfhood, expressing rhetorical equivalents of Pascal's and Baudelaire's spiritual vertigo, while patently engaged on a full-time and self-abnegating task.

Lowell modestly calls his book 'a small anthology of European poetry'. It is; and of course it is more than this. It is a meaningful design, in the centre of which stand the great nineteenth-century poems of self-devouring awareness: Leopardi's, Rimbaud's, Baudelaire's. First and last come poems whose subject is force: 'The Killing of Lykaon' (from the *Iliad*) chanting the force of destiny; 'Pigeons' (from Rilke) celebrating the force of gravity—two powers which embroil and ignore the narcissistic tragedies of man. In the beginning is:

> ' . . . the mania of Achilles
> that cast a thousand sorrows on the Greeks'

At the end is the 'mania to return', earthward, homeward, deathward.
   This is an impressive, disturbing work.

From *Essays in Criticism*, 13 (1963), 188-97.

C. CHADWICK

Meaning and Tone

WHAT, PRECISELY, does Robert Lowell mean when he says that, in his *Imitations*, he has been 'reckless with literal meaning but has laboured hard to get the tone'? All too often he seems, on the contrary, to labour hard to get the literal meaning, but fails to do so and, as a consequence, gets the tone wrong as well. In the opening verses of *Le Cygne*, for example, Baudelaire's chief concern is to evoke the hot, dry dustiness of the Paris street where the captive swan is dragging out its existence. The lines: 'la voirie Pousse un sombre ouragan dans l'air silencieux', refer to the rumble of dustcarts in the early morning and the word 'silencieux' clearly implies that it is the noise of a hurricane, not the rain it brings, that Baudelaire has in mind in using this metaphor. Lowell however fails to realise this and his version: 'a sprinkler spread a hurricane to lay the sediment', introduces a note of coolness and freshness which is quite out of key with the context.

Towards the end of the same poem he tries desperately hard to get the literal meaning of: 'Et tettent la Douleur comme une bonne louve', but, like Mr. Hill who mentions this line in his review in the April 1963 number of *Essays in Criticism,* instead of linking the simile with the object of the verb, he mistakenly links it with the subject: 'like wolf-nurses giving grief a tit to suck'. Consequently the tone of the line is radically altered so that it no longer conveys the utter hopelessness of those who have suffered so much and so long that they find solace in their own grief. Baudelaire expresses precisely the same idea in the preceding line when he describes such people as 'ceux qui s'abreuvent de pleurs', but again Lowell misses the point and transforms this passive resignation into an active, though unsuccessful, attitude to life in the phrase: 'waste their powers'.

As for the next and final verse of *Le Cygne* it is difficult to avoid the conclusion, on reading Lowell's version, that he has in fact missed the whole point of the poem. It is of course about captivity, about people exiled from their homeland; this is the common factor that links together the imprisoned swan, Andromache in the hands of Pyrrhus, and the negress Jeanne Duval longing to escape from the dismal cold of Paris. These individual examples lead up to, or rather widen out into, the sombre concluding lines:

> Je pense aux matelots oubliés dans une île,
> Aux captifs, aux vaincus . . . à bien d'autres encore!

Lowell's version however, by drowning the sailors whom Baudelaire has ship-
wrecked on a desert island, by presumably thinking of Jeanne Duval in her
capacity as a Paris prostitute rather than as an expatriate negress and by
introducing a new image which has nothing to do with the sorrows of captivity,
completely changes the significance of the conclusion and, in consequence, of
the poem as a whole:

> I think of Paris raising the white flag,
> drowned sailors, fallen girls . . . and many more!

An equally profound misunderstanding of the general tenor of another
poem, *Le Bateau Ivre,* no doubt explains the curious selection of verses which
make up Lowell's translation. The original poem is clearly divided into three
parts, the first seventeen verses telling of the fantastic sights Rimbaud has seen
on his largely imaginary travels, the next four expressing his surprise and
bewilderment that he should nevertheless nostalgically regret the stability of
the world of home, and the last four dealing with the difficult choice which
consequently faces him. These opposing forces in the poem are however
completely absent from Lowell's version and Rimbaud is transformed from an
adolescent on the threshold of life, longing to go on and yet tempted to turn
back, into an old sailor simply spinning yarns about his travels.

Regrettable though it may be that the key verse of *Le Bateau Ivre,* round
which the whole poem is built, should have been left out:

> Moi qui tremblais, sentant geindre à cinquante lieues
> Le rut des Béhémoths et les Maelstroms épais,
> Fileur éternal des immobilités bleues,
> Je regrette l'Europe aux anciens parapets!

at least this may be a better solution than translating key lines so incorrectly
that a poem is made to say the very opposite of what is meant. For this is what
has happened in Lowell's version of Mallarmé's *Toast Funèbre,* an elegy to
Théophile Gautier whose theme is that the man is dead but that the poet lives
on in his work. The pivot of the poem lies in the following lines:

> Est-il de ce destin rien qui demeure, non?
> O vous tous, oubliez une croyance sombre.
> Le splendide génie éternal n' a pas d'ombre.

But instead of keeping the first of these lines as a negative question to which
the implied answer is an affirmative, Lowell substitutes a full stop for Mallarmé's comma and thus completely reverses the meaning: 'Does anything remain
of this great claim? No'. Since this is difficult to reconcile with Mallarmé's
demand, in the next line, that any such gloomy thoughts should be banished,
Lowell's confusing solution seems to be to introduce an alien religious element

and to undermine the superbly confident tone of the third line by reducing genius to mere craft and by transforming its eternal splendour into false talent:

> Men, forget your narrow faiths, no shade
> darkens our métier's artificial fire.

To confuse the issue still further he later adds a line of his own as a prelude to the poem's concluding paragraph:

> His tombstone ornaments the garden path—
> here is the only true and lasting light . . .

Unfortunately however the whole point of the elegy is that the only true and lasting light is *not* beneath the tombstone but in Gautier's poetry, in the 'agitation solennelle par l'air de paroles', as Mallarmé describes it a few lines earlier where Lowell misses the essential word: 'paroles'.

In the light of these examples, to which several others could be added, Lowell's distinction between meaning and tone does not therefore seem to be a valid one. The two things are so inextricably bound together that failure to grasp the one inevitably leads to failure to convey the other, with the result that, at least as far as *Le Cygne, Le Bateau Ivre* and *Toast Funèbre* are concerned, *Imitations,* as imitations, cannot be considered successful, whatever their worth as original poems may be.

From *Essays in Cricicism,* 13 (1963), 432-35.

RICHARD POIRIER

For The Union Dead

ROBERT LOWELL is, by something like a critical consensus, the greatest American poet of the mid-century, probably the greatest poet now writing in English.

Consultant in Poetry at the Library of Congress three years after his first volume, *Land of Unlikeness* (1944); winner of the Pulitzer Prize for his second, *Lord Weary's Castle* (1946); of the National Book Award for *Life Studies* (1959) and of the Bollingen Translation Prize for *Imitations* (1961)—it might well seem, at first glance, that Lowell's is a poetic career, to quote Edmund Wilson, "on the old nineteenth-century scale." And yet, to recall the great figures of that period, the nearly legislative power and general popularity of Wordsworth, for instance, or to think of the more recent example of Frost, is to realize that the audience for Lowell's poetry is remarkably small, given the many public honors he has received, and quite special.

In fact, nothing attests so much to his originality as the fact that the very large public which has learned to read Yeats and Eliot and to appreciate Frost for something more than home-spun is not therefore prepared to cope very satisfactorily with Lowell. It isn't simply that his poems have come more and more to reveal a discomfort with the rhetorical and poetical modes of these earlier writers. Even more important, especially in understanding why Lowell hasn't captured even a large academic audience, is the fact that nothing he writes accommodates itself to the theories that allow us to make sense of the earlier poetry of the century—concepts about the nature of reality which teachers like to discuss when they are presumably discussing the poetry of Wallace Stevens and William Carlos Williams, or mythologies about the degeneracy of modern life derived from T. S. Eliot.

Probably the ambition of most poets is to create a new vulgarity, the vernacular and the assumptions that will govern the consciousness of a generation or two. Even people who have never read Frost can't stop by woods on a snowy evening, for example, without a nagging suspicion that their feelings are not perhaps entirely original, and many lines from early Eliot have by now the evocative power of lyrics from old blues: "I should have been a pair of ragged claws. . . . " It can be predicted with some confidence that none of Lowell's poems, many of them about breakdowns altogether more contemporary in their psychological immediacy than Prufrock's, will ever achieve the popularity of Eliot's "Love Song."

What I admire most about Lowell's poems, in fact, is that they seldom invite anyone to expand inside them; they almost never yield to generalizations about life or about the present situation; they stifle their own eloquence just at the point where it might publicize rather than serve a close scrutiny of the poet's feelings.

Take, for instance, the image that ends the title poem: "Everywhere,/ giant finned cars nose forward like fish;/ a savage servility/ slides by on grease." The image seems to be in the tradition of Eliotic cultural finickiness, except that the rhythms are glumly unmannered, wholly without the stressed satiric flippancy that Eliot brings to this kind of observation. In Lowell's poetry such images are never only about Other People. They are weighted with self-recognition, the lines in question reminding us of the earlier admission by the poet, when speaking of the gutted South Boston Aquarium, "I often sigh still/ for the dark downward and vegetating kindgom/ of the fish and reptile."

It is nearly impossible in Lowell's poetry to separate personal breakdown from the poet's visions of public or historical decline: in "Caligula," he looks at "the rusty Roman medal where I see/ my lowest depths of possibility." Giving this poetry an extraordinary air of personal authority is the assurance that the poet's most private experiences simply *are* of historical, even mythical, importance. Readers are perplexed by Lowell whenever they expect his poetry to "earn the right," as that horrid bit of critical cant would have it, to the connections between private and public significance which he chooses to take for granted.

Thus, while the personal mess in the poem "Night Sweat" is hellishly more than merely aristocratic slackness, the manner of describing it beautifully illustrates what might be called the aristocracy of Lowell's verse. There is a marked delay in arriving at the larger metaphors of the poem, an absence of metaphoric nervousness, of the poet saying, in effect, that what he is revealing about himself is really "like" something that is true of someone else or understandable in terms of some larger situation:

> Work-table, litter, books and standing lamp,
> plain things, my stalled equipment, the old broom—
> but I am living in a tidied room,
> for ten nights now I've felt the creeping damp
> float over my pajamas' wilted white . . .
> Sweet salt embalms me and my head is wet,
> everything streams and tells me this is right;
> my life's fever is soaking in night sweat—
> one life, one writing! But the downward glide
> and bias of existing wrings us dry—
> always inside me is the child who died,
> always inside me is his will to die—
> one universe, one body . . . in this urn
> the animal night sweats of the spirit burn.

The poem expands (for a moment to "us") and contracts ("one universe, one body"), but nothing personally preoccupying is adapted to the exigencies of clarification or to regularity of rhythm. The only summary of his personal history is his own body, the container which is also the thing contained. And "urn" is a brilliantly decisive choice for the concluding image of that body, describing at once a container for the ashes of the dead which is itself burnt clay.

This magnificent new collection exists in defiance of what the poems often seem to be saying: that there is no recourse from "night sweat" either in rhetoric or in the elucidation of metaphors. With its half-rhymes, its rhythms that get lost, its patterns of assonance that seem accidental, the verse suggests some faltering after an order, after a polish that cannot be achieved. At times, even the intensity of color given by memory to the past is rejected as a falsification:

> Remember? We sat on a slab of rock.
> From this distance in time,
> it seems the color
> of iris, rotting and turning purpler,
>
> but it was only
> the usual gray rock
> turning the usual green
> when drenched by the sea.

Here (the poem is called "Water") and in most of the love poems the pain of recollection is in the resistance to poetic coloring, to any sense-making order at all, of the things and persons of the past. Their bristling integrity nags at the poet's mind, as with the promise of symbolic or metaphoric significance, and it is of course this same integrity which prevents that promise from being redeemed.

Lowell is a poet of great tenderness for things and people and for the human body. In this and in other ways he shares some of the unique distinctions that have set D. H. Lawrence apart from most writers in this century. His tenderness derives, in so far as the derivation can be located in his work, from the discovery he keeps making that persons and things are not something else, something larger. They are vulnerable, mysteriously alone and physically fragile in what they are. "Alfred Corning Clark" is an example in this volume of a gentleness that comes from refusing to do to a person what poetic elegies usually try to do to them. The poem so cherishes the details of the man that it offers nothing like a finished portrait of him: "There must be something," the poet reflects, and, a bit later, "I owe you something. . . . "

Among the poems that are most revealing about Lowell is one simply entitled, "Hawthorne." His interest in this earlier American writer is perhaps predictable, and it will get further expression with the production this season of three of Hawthorne's stories adapted by Lowell for the stage. For one thing, Hawthorne belongs to the history of early 19th-century New England with which Lowell feels a familial closeness. For another, he imagines Hawthorne entrapped much as is the poet himself among evidences of a past that promise but will not yield their secrets:

> The disturbed eyes rise,
> furtive, foiled, dissatisfied
> from meditation on the true
> and insignificant.

Perhaps most importantly, Hawthorne is obsessed with the kind of inner turmoil that has characterized Lowell's poetry, in a variety of ways, from the beginning. It got expressed earlier as a conflict between Roman Catholicism, to which Lowell was at one time converted, and a New England Calvinism which is part of his heritage. (The longest poem in the present volume, and not, I think, one of the best, is "Jonathan Edwards in Western Massachusetts.") But with *The Mills of the Kavanaughs* in 1958 and later with *Life Studies*, Lowell gave an increasing and very rewarding emphasis to a kind of domestic biography and autobiography.

Through all this, the poetry has continued to reveal a Hawthornean struggle among the "laws" that compete within the poet's nature. These "laws" are a kind of imposition from the history which has shaped him, offering the only alternatives, and by no means satisfying ones, to an always threatening "lawless" collapse in the face of stress or agony. The poem entitled "Law," the most enigmatic in this volume, seems to be precisely about this dilemma. The past, none of which he can reject or scarcely forget, exerts a control on his imagination, and his imagination, even while working to discover new and liberating possibilities in itself, can only be kept sane by reaching some understanding with the past.

This recurrent problem in Lowell's poetry receives here one of its most beautiful expressions in "The Neo-Classical Urn." It is a recollection of youthful callousness which the poet recognizes his kinship both with "turtles" and with the "urn" in which, as a child, he threw them to suffer and die. The discovery of this metaphorical connection is itself the subject of the poem, as startling to the poet as it is to us. The poet as "turtle," with "No/ grace, no cerebration," and as a neo-classical urn in which the animals die is a reminder of "Night Sweat": " . . . in this urn/ the animal night sweats of the spirit burn." But within this burning and misery of mind that can conjure up such associations, the poet is finally able to appeal to "laws" created in the past by the poetic imagination: the heroic couplet that ends the poem with a neo-classical order and restraint upon the terrifying vision it contains:

> nothings! Turtles! I rub my skull,
> that turtle shell,
> and breathe their dying smell,
> still watch their crippled last survivors pass,
> and hobble humpbacked through the grizzled grass.

More than any contemporary writer, poet or novelist, Lowell has created the language, cool and violent all at once, of contemporary introspection. He is our truest historian. He evokes the past not as if it alone were history but as if its meaning exists necessarily in its relation to that more important element of history which is himself, now and here; and he confronts literature, as he does in *Imitations,* not again, as something that belongs to the past but that belongs to him, taking in him some special shape which can then be given to us.

Because of such poems as the 35 that are collected here, we are allowed to take these days for something better than they are. Robert Frost once wrote that "There is at least so much good in the world that it admits of form and the making of form. . . . Anyone who has achieved the least form to be sure of it, is lost to the larger excruciations. . . . The artist, the poet, might be expected to be the most aware of such assurance, but it is really everybody's sanity to feel it and live by it."

That was 30 years ago, and such assurances are not now easier to come by. Lowell never takes his "form" from other writers who, in the face of their own time and circumstances, suffered to achieve it from themselves. Instead, the form of any given poem emerges from something increasingly rare in poetry or in life: from a suffering spirit seeking not ease but a further confrontation with precisely those degradations in the self and in the times that are a challenge to form and to assurance.

From *Book Week,* 11 Oct. 1964, pp. 1, 16.

CHRISTOPHER RICKS

The Three Lives of Robert Lowell

THE SINGULAR strength of Robert Lowell's poetry has always been a matter of his power to enforce a sense of context. He has been determined, as few poets have been, to face the implications of the dramatic monologue, the only new poetic kind of any importance for centuries and the one which has established itself as peculiarly apt for the modern poet. A sense of context becomes a point of urgency, because otherwise a dramatic monologue will be merely a speech from a missing play. Lowell's gift has been to bring a sense of context to bear upon his poems, not just in local effects but as a whole. And the best poems in *For the Union Dead* go beyond their predecessors precisely in their ability to enforce simultaneously the three contexts which in Lowell's earlier work had tended to get hived into separate poems.

First, his personal experience, an 'I' who really does live here and now and who comes across as individual and yet not idiosyncratic. Second, the way we live now, a social and political web in which 'the Republic summons Ike', and underground parking is gouged out beneath Boston Common, and bombs may and indeed do go off. Third, the outer context, historical, literary and religious, dealing with the old unhappy things which are not far off, the diverse deaths of Jesus, Caligula and Mussolini.

The achievement of this new volume is manifest in a fact which could be misread as a lack of focus: the fact that the book is not predominantly identified with any one of the three contexts that have always both liberated and chan nelled Lowell's imagination. *Imitations,* by its nature as free-standing translation, was committed only to enforcing a historical and literary context. 'Only', not because that is a trivial thing, but because the decision entailed leaving out quite a lot of Lowell. That Lowell's French was corrected by T. S. Eliot was no substitute. *Imitations* may be in one sense a more sharply focused book than *For the Union Dead*— but in a lesser sense. Similarly with *Life Studies,* a collection which included poems of various modes (historical monologues, and 'Inauguration Day: January 1953') but which was predominantly devoted to poems of a personal context: those piercing and affectionate poems about Lowell's own pains and those of his family. *Life Studies* was, after all, Lowell's title for both the volume and for this, the main section. Faber managed to disguise this emphasis (as well as to deprive Englishmen of an important work by Lowell) by omitting from the English edition '91 Revere St.', 36 pages of reminiscential prose which confirmed the emphasis as central to *Life Studies* (poems which are mainly studies in death).

For the Union Dead does not represent any dramatic break. All along, Lowell has written poems which embody the three contexts. But hitherto each collection had tended to manifest an emphasis which was also something of an exclusion. (In the earliest poems, Roman Catholicism was inclined to upstage the others.) And hitherto he had not managed to write many poems in which justice was done to all three, each worthy of the others in their convergence. The sheer distinction of the present title-poem (like that of 'Fall 1961', 'Florence', and the reprinted 'Beyond the Alps') comes from its marrying the three sources of Lowell's imagination—and of our own. 'For the Union Dead' outdoes the previous poems, and by multiplying them, not adding. Its setting is 'the Old South Boston Aquarium' together with the statues of Colonel Shaw and his infantry. The personal context is established at once, with a childhood memory of the Aquarium, a memory later to be hideously distorted or parodied:

> Once my nose crawled like a snail on the glass;
> my hand tingled
> to burst the bubbles
> drifting from the noses of the cowed, compliant fish.

The social, civic and political context defines itself by contrast both with this memory (the Aquarium is now derelict) and with the historical memory of what Shaw and his soldiers represented.

> There are no statues for the last war here;
> on Boyleston Street, a commercial photograph
> shows Hiroshima boiling
> over a Mosler Safe, the 'Rock of Ages'
> that survived the blast

The audacity of 'Boyleston . . . boiling' is an attempt to match the effrontery of the photograph itself, with the trade-name accomplishing, gratuitously, all that Lowell could ask *sub specie aeternitatis*. The poem is superbly organised and yet wonderfully free, so that to point to its bubble-imagery, say, is to schematise rawly. It finally circles back to its memory of childhood, at which there dawns, unvoiced, the fear that the Aquarium's tanks are now dry because the sea-world has broken loose:

> The Aquarium is gone. Everywhere,
> giant finned cars nose forward like fish;
> a savage servility
> slides by on grease.

The accurate and the suggestive here combine, permitting Lowell to intimate without pretentiousness that humanity is preying on itself like monsters of the deep. How right to eschew a hyphen in 'giant finned'. And there is an equivocation (itself sliding) in 'slides by on grease', where 'on', used here as it is of cars, suggests ('runs on oil') that grease is the fuel as well as what you slide on, both the internal motive-power and the external slippery slope.

In its relating of the internal and the external, as of the personal, the political and the historical, 'For the Union Dead' is one of the finest poems Lowell has written. And if it is about sea-monsters we remember the urgent cry in one of the other poems: 'Pity the monsters!' Lowell—and it is the crown—does persuade us of his pity. If, like many other people, he sees in present-day America some desolating illness, his tone is very different from that in which Allen Tate spoke when introducing Lowell's first book of poems. For Tate in 1944, Lowell was to be warmly contrasted with 'the democratic poets who enthusiastically greet the advent of the slave-society.' Lowell's recent work holds no brief for the right of Southern gentlemen to impugn only one kind of 'slave-society'. Nor are Lowell's poems so sure that what America is suffering from is an excess of democracy.

'Caligula' shows another meeting of the three. Its starting point, as with all poems, is arbitrary: the fact that as a child Lowell gained (chose?) the nickname Caligula:

> My namesake, Little Boots, Caligula,
> you disappoint me. Tell me what I saw
> to make me like you when we met at school?

The whole poem unfolds that altogether convincing hesitation in 'like you'—a verb or not? Does Lowell like Caligula or is he like him? The latter possibility is cunningly held open, with an unobstrusiveness which shows Lowell's mature confidence. The success of the poem comes from the fusion of the personal anecdote with the historical and political.

Historical, because of the passionate skill with which we are shown Caligula's appalling life and death. (Lowell has always found in Rome a combination of the marmoreal and the frenzied which permits him to use a true hyperbole.) Political, because even if Caligula was in one sense 'the last Caligula' (its closing words), there have been other such men. The political, historical and personal meet in the psychopathology of Caligula, and Lowell has seized a setting which demands a violence which elsewhere could be suspect:

> You hear your household panting on all fours,
> and itemise your features—sleep's old aide!
> *Item:* your body hairy, badly made,
> head hairless, smoother than your marble head;
> *Item:* eyes hollow, hollow temples, red
> cheeks rough with rouge, legs spindly, hands that leave
> a clammy snail's trail on your soggy sleeve . . .
> a hand no hand will hold . . . nose thin, thin neck—
> you wish the Romans had a single neck!

The shrieking inarticulacy of that last famous wish (embodied in the mad rhyme of 'neck' with 'neck') springs out in murderous contrast to the itemising of features, and Lowell manages to make us remember, because the poem is both then and now, that nuclear war has indeed given us all one neck. One might add that Lowell's quotation makes use of the very strong anti-democratic feelings which lunge impatiently through American life today, and yet doesn't yield to those feelings.

It is not unimportant that the lines by Lowell so much resemble the great poetry of Jonson's *Sejanus*, the opening speech of which itemises the human features in a way which similarly suggests a disintegration in Rome that is at once spiritual, physical and social:

> We have no shift of faces, no cleft tongues,
> No soft and glutinous bodies that can stick
> Like snails on painted walls.

The comparison with Jonson's tragedies, here and elsewhere (cp. Lowell's translation of *Phèdre*), deserves to be demonstrated at length. Both can write with a physical force about the body politic. (*For the Union Dead* is a grimly punning title.) Both are masters of the glacial, the heated and the poisonous, and both create a poetry which is profoundly classical in its memory of dignity and yet profoundly of its time in its sense of turbulence. Jonson would not have despised the couplet:

> You stare down hallways, mile on stoney mile,
> Where statues of the gods return your smile.

The assurance manifest in the unsignalled pun on "stare down" (as the couplet unrolls, the suggestion becomes Gorgonian); the way the couplet congeals around 'stoney'; the chilling force here given to the cliché 'return your smile' (not the reciprocity of love, in the circumstances); and the explicit feeling of vista'd repetition which is enforced by the near-identity of the rhyme 'mile'/ 'smile'—all these show a technical mastery that is inseparable from imaginative mastery.

With the straight historical poems Lowell now seems rather less happy. There was a fine monologue in *Life Studies*. 'The Banker's Daughter', in which Marie de Medici speaks 'shortly after' the assassination of her husband, Henri IV'. One of the new poems, 'Lady Ralegh's Lament, 1618', invites comparison but then finds itself snubbed—Lady Ralegh is inferior, and not just socially. There is a real problem about historical allusiveness: how much can Lowell legitimately expect us to know? And if he expects us to know quite a lot, what happens when there swims into mind a famous historical anecdote which Lowell apparently would prefer excluded, Lady Ralegh begins 'Sir Walter, oh, oh, my own Sir Walter'. If it is the case that those are her very words they nevertheless remain uncomfortably close to Aubrey's notorious anecdote about Ralegh:

He loved a wench well: and one time getting up one of the Mayds of Honour up against a tree in a Wood ('twas his first Lady) who seemed at first boarding to be something fearfull of her Honour, and modest, she cryed, sweet Sir Walter, what doe you me ask? Will you undoe me? Nay, sweet Sir Walter! Sweet Sir Walter! At last, as the danger and the pleasure at the same time grew higher, she cryed in the extasey, Swisser Swatter Swisser Swatter.

Allusiveness creates problems for Lowell. Is a line like 'I dabble in the dapple of the day' in any way making use of our awareness that it is Spelt from Hopkins' Leaves? Nor is the problem less when the allusions are to quotations previously quoted in Lowell's own work. 'Jonathan Edwards in Western Massachusetts' has a few touching moments—though it does occasionally sound like a kind of Jonathan Edwards Revisited. But what about this?

> you saw the spiders fly,
>
> basking at their ease,
> swimming from tree to tree—

Lowell-lovers will already have leaped to their feet to intone the unforgettable opening of 'Mr Edwards and the Spider':

> I saw the spiders marching through the air,
> Swimming from tree to tree that mildewed day . . .

The simply historical poems seem to have suffered an attenuation, most apparent in the sentimentality of 'Hawthorne'. Written for a centenary edition, the poem 'draws heavily on prose sentences' by Hawthorne, which does not justify the fungoid phrasing.

From *The New Statesman*, 26 March 1965, pp. 496-97.

ROBERT BRUSTEIN

The Old Glory

Benito Cereno is the third play in the extraordinary theater trilogy by Robert
Lowell called *The Old Glory,* a work in which the renowned poet has fashioned
a dramatic history of the American character. Held together by the unifying
symbol of the flag, *The Old Glory* is based on stories by Hawthorne and a
novella by Melville, but while Mr. Lowell has managed to adapt these tales
with relative fidelity to the original texts, he has made them wholly and
uniquely his own work. Invested with the author's keen historical sense and
marvelous gift for language, the source materials assume the thickness and
authority of myth; ritual and metaphors abound; traditional literature and
historical events begin to function like Greek mythology, as the source and
reflection of contemporary behavior. Mr. Lowell feels the past working in his
very bones. And it is his subtle achievement not only to have evoked this past,
but also to have superimposed the present upon it, so that the plays manage
to look forward and backward at the same time. Adopting a style which is
purposely chilling, measured and remote, he has endowed his plays with flinty
intelligence and tautened passion, making them work on the spectator with all
the suggestive power of non-discursive poems.

The three plays examine the American character at three different points in
its historical development. This character the author finds to be permeated with
violence from its beginnings—a violence which invariably erupts out in moments of panic. In *Endecott and the Red Cross,* a mild-mannered Puritan military
man, faced with high-living Anglican-Royalists in colonial America, is forced
into shedding blood by political-religious expediency; and in *My Kinsman
Major Molineux,* the American Revolution unfolds as a violent nightmare
experienced by two Deerfield youths seeking out their British cousin in Boston,
"the city of the dead."

In *Benito Cereno,* the third and finest play, Mr. Lowell brings us to the
beginning of the 19th century and proceeds to unearth the seeds of our current
discords. Based on Herman Melville's novella of the same name, *Benito Cereno*
has all the theatrical power of the first two plays, as well as a heavily charged
prose style and a strong suspenseful narrative. Melville's story is largely concerned with the shadow cast over a civilized mind by the primitive darkness.
Mr. Lowell heightens this theme, examining along the way the ambiguous
American attitude towards slavery and servitude.

In the American Place Theatre production, Jonathan Miller, the director,
paced this play with an eye to its half-languorous, half-ominous atmosphere,

giving it the rhythm of "an ocean undulating in long scoops of swells," but finally letting it explode into a shocking climax, to the accompaniment of discharging muskets. The visual effects of the original production, with its simple set and illustrative costuming, were excellent (the crisp uniforms of the American officers in black cutaway coats and white tights juxtaposed against the shabby-sumptuous attire of Cereno and the rags of the slaves). But it is the acting that was really unusual. In an age of flaccid, self-indulgent histrionics, Mr. Miller evoked performances of extraordinary depth, control and energy. Three actors in particular were superb: Roscoe Lee Browne, alternating between Calypso sunniness and sinister threat as Babu; Lester Rawlins, suave, smug and self-satisfied as Delano; and Frank Langella as Cereno, his eyes continually lowered with shame, his voice morose and rich, a trembling wreck of stateliness and nobility. But it is a violation to single out individuals for praise when the entire cast was functioning with that precision and power that we have come to expect only from long-established repertory companies.

The Old Glory, certainly, is the first American play to utilize historical materials in a compelling theatrical manner (just compare it with those lifeless high-school pageants that Maxwell Anderson used to grind out), perhaps because it is the first such play to assume a mature intellect on the part of its audience. After years of prosaic language, mundane forms and retarded themes—obstacles which only O'Neill was able to transcend successfully in his last plays, and then only through sheer doggedness and will—the American drama has finally developed an important subject and an eloquent voice. The Old Glory may well mark the beginning of a dramatic renaissance in America, during which our theater—like our fiction and poetry—will be able to tap the sources of our inmost being, and not just sink us deeper into narcosis and complacency. Benito Cereno is a cultural-poetic masterpiece, but the entire trilogy is an event of great moment. For it heralds the arrival not just of a brilliant new dramatist but of one who may very well come to revolutionize the American theater.

From The Old Glory (New York: Farrar, Straus & Giroux, 1965), pp. xi-xiv.

JOHN SIMON

Strange Devices on the Banner

THE OLD GLORY. By Robert Lowell. Illustrated. Farrar, Straus & Giroux. 194 pp. $4.95.

THERE IS always joy in certain quarters when a poet starts writing for the theater. In the glorious ages of the drama, from Aeschylus to Goethe and Schiller, drama and poetry lived in wedlock. The 19th century broke up that happy union. But sentimentalists like to see marriages last, however unviable they have become, and there seems to be less rejoicing in heaven over a repentant sinner than on earth over reconciled spouses. So, when Robert Lowell's *The Old Glory* was produced off-Broadway, when, in other words, a major American poet was appearing on the stage with verse drama, it was to some—notably to most of the highbrow critics—as if the world had suddenly become a better place.

The Old Glory consists of three one-acters: two shorter ones, *Endecott and the Red Cross* and *My Kinsman, Major Molineux,* based on short stories by Hawthorne, and one longer one, *Benito Cereno,* from Melville's novella. In *Endecott,* a well-meaning Puritan governor of Salem in the 1630s discovers, as he quashes mixed Indian-and-white maypole dancing, that, much as he is against King Charles and the Church of England and their various worldly and opportunistic representatives in the New World, he is not really for the more fanatical aspects of his own Puritans. Yet he is forced into severity against the revelers because "a statesman can either work with merciless efficiency, and leave a desert,/or he can work in a hit and miss fashion/and leave a cess-pool." Endecott opts for the desert, but allows for a little bit of cesspool by way of an oasis.

In *Molineux,* a youth from Deerfield arrives in Boston with his little brother just before Tea Party time. He hopes for a career through his powerful kinsman who commands the redcoats in Boston. During a hallucinatory night in which the Bostonians treat the boys with a mixture of hostility and mockery, the Major is always mysteriously alluded to and strangely unseeable—until the boys have to watch him being killed by the anti-English mob, and are even hypnotically drawn into that mob.

The plot of *Benito Cereno* needs no summary, but it should be noted that Lowell has made considerable changes here (as elsewhere), mostly in the direction of showing the contradictions in the American attitude toward Ne-

groes: "In a civilized country," says Lowell's Captain Delano, "everyone disbe-
lieves in slavery and wants slaves." And the play proceeds to show the rights
and wrongs of both blacks and whites.

Clearly, Lowell is trying to capture the ironies, cruelties, and inconclusive-
ness on which America was built: in *Endecott,* the ambiguities are chiefly
religious; in *Molineux,* political; in *Cereno,* racial. Beyond that, though, he is
concerned with essential human nature, which he sees as paradoxical, untrust-
worthy, and, above all, tenebrose. But, regrettably, there are three obstacles he
cannot quite negotiate: the limitations of the one-acter, the demands of dramatic form, the problem of stage poetry.

Endecott, for example, is an interesting figure who manages to arouse our
sympathetic curiosity, but only at the expense of swallowing up most of the
playlet: his psyche exacts much more of our attention than do the perfunctory
characters and negligible events of the play. In *Cereno,* attempts at writing some
sequences in the manner of Genet, Beckett or Kafka rub uneasily against
patches of realism and even a Hollywoodish, shoot-em-up finale. In *Molineux,*
the absurdist mode is fairly consistent (though not so witty as in Beckett or
Ionesco), but it clashes with stabs at mythologizing—Charon is introduced as
ferryman to Boston, "the City of the Dead"!—and, throughout, one feels a
certain confusion between symbol and rigmarole.

Again, dramatizing fiction has required such devices as the confidant, but,
in *Molineux,* the presence of the kid brother is not only illogical, it also
dissipates the harrowing isolation of Hawthorne's solitary youth. In *Cereno,*
Lowell must supply Captain Delano with a sidekick, the naive bosun Perkins,
whom the poet intended both as butt of Delano's greater insight and wit and
as a Prince Hal, who is supposed to end up, as Lowell put it in an interview,
"superior to Delano." This superiority is meant to manifest itself, Lowell tells
us, in two short and separate speeches, one of which is only six words long
and, allegedly, hinges on Perkins' ironic use of the one word "Sir."

Now this sort of thing is all very well in lyric poetry, but it just does not
register in performed drama. And it is true of all three plays that, though they
are aware of the things that make a play a play—not merely action and conflict,
as commonly held, but also diversified verbal texture, humor, pathos, variety
of tempo, absorbing talk, and so on—he is unable either to provide enough
of them or to marshal them properly. Thus action tends to bunch up in one
place, humor to sound forced, and the language to become static or inconsistent.
Babu, for example, far from remaining a slave fresh out of Africa, turns into
a Calypso cut-up and connoiseur of American and European history and conditions.

Yet the final problem is the poetry itself. Though written in free verse, *The
Old Glory* attains to poetry only in Captain Delano's speech beginning "I see
an ocean undulating in long scoops and swells . . . " But this passage is only
a slight reworking of Melville's third paragraph; and where it departs from
Melville's prose, it improves on it only in one participle, "swallows sabering
flies." Here now is a typical passage:

Things aren't really bad,
but the time will come, the time will surely come,
I know the King's mind, or rather the mind of his advisers—
kings can't be said to have minds.
The rulers of England will revoke our charter,
they will send us a royal Governor,
they will quarter soldiers on us,
they will impose their system of bishops.

What is the point of printing this as verse? Even its most eloquent champion, Robert Brustein, refers to it in the Introduction as a "prose style." True, there is the precedent of Eliot and Fry, but are *The Cocktail Party* and *Venus Observed* worthy of emulation? Verse that is not really verse can add only pretentiousness to a play, confuse the actors, and throw dust in the ears of the audience. It may even deflect the playwright's attention from his primary task.

But could one not write truly poetic plays today? The answer, apparently, is no. By far the best 20th-century poet-playwright, Bertolt Brecht, kept his poetry off the stage. On it, he allowed for song interludes; otherwise, with trifling exceptions, his plays were in prose. Poetry today has, unfortunately, become a minority art, no longer an integral part of the culture as it was in the heyday of verse drama. Reluctantly, we must accept its divorce from the theater, which must at least *seem* to speak the language of the land. The poet, as writer, may still have a place in the theater; poetry, barring a miracle, does not. What history hath put asunder, no man is likely to join together.

From *Book Week,* 20 Feb. 1966, pp. 4, 12.

JONATHAN PRICE

Prometheus Bound

IN *Prometheus Bound* Lowell continues his self-examination under the shadow of philosophy: the play is dry, difficult, metaphysical; it is, somehow, the paradigm of what is worst in Lowell, and by Lowell's peculiar nature, what is best in him. Critics try in vain to avoid its value: shining icon or wretched embarassment, the play will not be forgotten, as long as Lowell's poems are read. For it is a brief philosophy, a lesson in his dialectic, more, it is an intense moral, intellectual, and emotional criticism of his own life and his world. . . .

One reason that *Prometheus* continues to bother us, and makes us sustain doubts about it long after the performance, is Lowell's strategy of setting up conflicts within the play, and then, while appearing to resolve them, he refuses to commit himself too completely to either side, even at the very end of the play. He progresses by opposites.

This, of course, is an old method for him; beginning in his earliest poems, Lowell confesses an open admiration for the Metaphysicals and a fondness for complexity and paradox. "Each poem was more difficult than the one before, and had more ambiguity." In this play, in line after line, we find Lowell refusing to settle for the simple statement, changing it, recasting it so that it will be more accurate—and therefore more involved. This kind of sensibility is at work when he writes lines like, "He turned our appetites to duties." Or, "No one else can bear up the world. Atlas cannot bear it—because he cannot, he must." What a net of thinking is meshed in those short phrases.

In early poems, like 'Our Lady of Walsingham,' or 'Colloquy at Black Rock,' Lowell would take some subject, and contemplate it so long that it gradually took on more significance and symbolized many more things for him than it did at the start. The black mud in 'Colloquy at Black Rock,' for instance, comes to suggest St. Paul, St. Stephen, Hawthorne's vision of evil, the water that Christ walked on, and the soul of man lacking charity. The religious overtones hint where this method came from: it is in many ways the method of religious contemplation recommended by St. Bernard and St. Bonaventure. In the 'forties, Lowell's aim was partly to achieve this 'mystical Union' with God, but, now, after rejecting the method in pursuit of more objective truths about himself, he has taken it up again.

Whereas in the early poems he chose a concrete incident in order to pile

on mythic references, in *Prometheus Bound,* he chooses the myth because it
opens up so much of his real experience. In his youth, Lowell often began
seeming to hope the world would turn out to be all good or all bad (in which
case he could feel justified for assaulting it, with all of a pacifist's fury at the
betrayal), but discovering that it was not that simple, he would write in short
taut lines that turned in on themselves, attacking, and unbalancing each other.
Paradox is the style of men who would like to see clearly, but see too clearly
for that.

And now that he is trying to feel his way toward truth,—about himself and
about God—he seems to have realized how useful this old thick style could
be, particularly as a vehicle for his hero, Prometheus, who is continually
thinking out loud, trying to reason and argue and bull his way into some kind
of understanding of what is going on around him and in his own mind. At
one point, he has Prometheus say, "I was trying to feel my way toward truth.
One word led to another." The chorus makes a move, as if to interrupt, but
he shouts, "No, don't check me, I have little faith now, but I still look for
truth, some momentary crumbling foothold."

In an autobiographical passage a little farther on, Lowell has Prometheus
admit that he has always tried to find this always-disappearing shadow, this
'truth.' "I think I may have either known or hoped or something once.
. . . I forgot when. I remember hunting for . . . what shall I call them? Causes,
knots, heads of action? I was a savage head-hunter then, always hot on the trail
of powers I hoped to defeat and tame and put to work. You would be mistaken,
though, if you thought I was looking for domestic animals or human slaves—
these powers were invisible, though meaningful, I never saw one.

"I saw nothing except some hole, light through some slit, some eye that
wasn't an eye, but the eye of a needle, forever withdrawing and narrowing, and
winking derisively. Everything was held in the grip of something else. I was
on a fool's errand, and yet I was guided by the great gods of that day, their
most powerful flashes and later by the steady light of my own mind. That mind
was in no way walled in or useless. Each thought was like a finger touching,
tampering, testing, and trying to give things a little of my bias to alter and
advance."

It is clear that Lowell does not believe now that such truth is ever genuinely
found, but he does make a hero of the man who continues to search for it,
even when all illusion of success has fallen away. That, in fact, constitutes the
basic action of this play. Prometheus, rejecting any idea of union with the
godhead, nevertheless wants that union with oneself which is known as truth
or, at least, honesty. He battles to be true to his own experience of things and
to formulate it honestly; he is fighting to see things clearly. But that is
intimately bound up in the problem of saying them clearly to himself and to
his almost unnoticed audience of minor characters, so we also feel the struggle
for expression. These two battles—of a mind wrestling toward clarity— shape
the main course of the play. They involve us in a series of ambiguities and
internal conflicts which go much deeper than mere stylistic wordplay.

For Prometheus is trying to find out the truth about his relationship to power, and power, especially as Lowell thought about the situation with Prometheus the victim and Zeus the apparent tormentor, takes many more shapes than Aeschylus thought of. Lowell takes as his cue Camus' *Caligula* and Sartre's *The Flies*.

Lowell's 'existentialism' has never been very whole-hearted. It is more the despair of a platonist who cannot find any Ideas behind the cave; no matter how hard he looks, the world is an abyss. Nothing is there. But Lowell does not sense how this could free him. True, he has no authority to answer to and can therefore do whatever he desires; true, he is not created by or for anyone, neither his parents, his state, nor his god, and therefore he can create his own life. But Lowell does not take that step. About all he will commit himself to is a rather dim affirmation, as in 'Skunk Hour.'

"My night," he said, concerning that poem, "is not gracious, but secular, puritan, and agnostical. An Existentialist night." That is pretty much his idea of existentialism. The old order is destroyed; Platonism, and its ally, neo-platonic Christian mysticism, no longer seem true to him. In a way, *Prometheus Bound* is set in that dark light: to continue what he was saying about 'Skunk Hour.' "Somewhere in my mind was a passage from Sartre or Camus about reaching some point of final darkness where the one free act is suicide. Out of this comes the march and affirmation, an ambiguous one, of my skunks in the last two stanzas."

The destruction is there, in this play, and the affirmation too—though again, it seems insidiously ambiguous. Lowell has cleared away the immortality of the gods—they die, fall into decay, and in the end there is nothing but the void; endless entropy devouring itself. And Lowell himself seems at times to be declaring his own freedom in writing the play, as when he suggests that man can rebel and make himself into a kind of god, by thought. And the whole structure of the play is, after all, one of existential rejection of the inauthentic and the super-imposed.

At times, Prometheus himself is an existentialist rebel; he sees that Zeus can have no power over him if he will not allow it; he casts off all authority other than his own; he sees that "Now that I am chained here, I suppose I am almost free at last. You look on me as an insect, but you can't harness an insect like an ox and force it to haul your cart of stones. I won't answer your questions." Like Orestes in Sartre's *The Flies*, he realizes that he is free, "I was like a man who's lost his shadow. And there was nothing left in heaven, no right or wrong, nor anyone to give me orders."

And Zeus, at times, sounds very much like Caligula, the mad Emperor who saw that only one man could be entirely free at any one time and decided he would be the one: "Only Zeus is free," Prometheus says at one point, echoing the underlings in Camus' play talking about their own ruler. "Who has seen the mind of Zeus? He makes his own laws. They are hard. If he thinks at all of the gods who ruled before him, he thinks with contempt, and is silent." Prometheus compares himself to Zeus, pointing out how free Zeus is, "We have laws; God alone has motives."

But even Zeus's freedom is cut short by death. He too will fall. The sheer fact of decay prevents anyone from being completely free. And in a curious way, with this intrusion of death, we find ourselves back in a rather platonic universe. We take an almost scientific view: man seems free, but he is not. In the end he is squashed by his environment.

For Zeus is a god mired in platonism. By this I mean the 'essentialism' which Heidegger opposes to his own 'existentialism,' and, in addition, the more traditional neo-platonism, with its trappings of heavenly spheres, shadow caves, all-pervasive intellect, natural gradations from Ideal to real, and its affection for pure order. For Zeus is "terrified by anarchy"; he "cannot rest from trampling down chaos." He is creating the neo-platonic universe.

Prometheus too helped build that world. He and Zeus fought together against "the criminal chaos of Cronus," and after their victory, "Each god was given his place and function; no more over-lapping offices, no entangled wires, heads were rolling." In addition, Prometheus gave man the drug that Beckett attacks so vehemently in *Waiting for Godot* and *Endgame:* "I have given the sufferers a drug. Now they often forget about dying."

"How was that possible? What drug?"

"I gave them hope, blind hopes. When one blind hope lifts, another drifts down to replace it. Men see much less surely now, but they suffer less—they can hardly draw breath now, without taking hope." Of course, Prometheus sees that this hope is only a "consoling blindness." He himself sees, with the existentialists, that there is no hope, either in Ideas, or in Heaven, or in God's grace.

But, like a neurotic whose work never brings him any of the rewards he secretly expects, Prometheus will never abandon his own quest. For all that he sees it is useless. Lowell seems to see something heroic in this, and there is, in its muddle-headed way; it is at least an accurate picture of most men in our world today. For Prometheus still cherishes his own kind of 'hope' in an imaginary world.

"I had a vision. I saw the head of Cronus was a slab of meat, and it seemed to me if I could cut through the slab of meat, I would find a silver ball. The ball was there, it cracked open, inside it another, and another and another, and then suddenly the head of Cronus, my own head, and the heads of all the gods were broken spheres, all humming and vibrating with silver wires. The whole world was an infinite sphere of intelligence." Ah Plato, Plato.

And Prometheus, accepting the unreal world (Lowell himself points out that there is no mind at the back of things, only a slow acid eating like fire at the framework of the world), also accepts the premise that he ought to search out the truth, for it might be discoverable, at least in this world of order and definition which he envisions. "Around some bend, under some moving stone, behind some thought, if it were ever the right thought, I will find my key. No, not just another of Nature's million petty clues, but a key, *my key, the key,* the one that must be there, because it can't be there."

Because he keeps searching for that 'clue' that will unlock the universe, the clue that he knows is not there, this atheist saint, this Santayana ("There is no God, and Mary is his Mother") cannot entirely free himself from the belief that there may in fact be some larger order ruling everything. It may only be entropy, but even that gives us some sense of movement, some gradual falling off. It places man. And it prevents him from feeling entirely free of consequence and command.

Prometheus never genuinely believed revolt was possible. "We shared the same hopes. Something might be done, you thought, if fire could be given to man. Something could be done! No, you thought the sky would open for him. I was more despondent. I knew what would follow." And even for himself, what has he done? As the chorus says, "Feverish earth images spurt and crackle through your poor mind—so much done for man, so little for yourself!" If he had been a little more "loyal to the idiocy of things, or bolder, or more careless," he might have succeeded in his revolt; but as it was, "I had no choice, such was the gravity and devotion that drew me on."

Still, he did rebel. And that is more than most of the gods have done. Each of the three characters who come to visit Prometheus has given in to Zeus: Hermes is an arrogant sycophant; Io a helpless woman; Ocean a reformed revolutionary. Of the three, Ocean gives us the sharpest picture of what a young Turk like Prometheus might have done with his life.

In those days, Ocean and Prometheus planned to thwart Zeus, giving fire to man. But "Our hopes were noble exercises for the mind. Why did you put them into action? Action in that direction is only suffering. Give in to Zeus." As Ocean says, he wants to become the servant of the gods, to be part of their order. Prometheus scorns him, "I see your eyes are hurt by the glare of these rocks, you don't like to stand in the open." He accuses Ocean of wanting to wade back into Plato's protective cavern: "Already, you are furtively glancing over your shoulder, as if you longed for that dark rabbit-warren of rock-roofed caves I helped you build." Ocean urges surrender. But, as Prometheus says, his own revolt has brought him here. "I am lifted as high as I can go. You advise me to become like clay in the hands of God—advice that drags me lower down than the ooze and water from which I was born." Shaking his head, Ocean retreats to his undertow.

The chorus too is appalled, "We could never bear your punishment, or live with the thoughts that clash through your clear mind." For Prometheus is being punished not for what he has done as much as for what he has dared think. The chorus taunts—and Lowell does too—and Prometheus himself echoes their word, "Why do you go on believing you have done something? You have only proved Zeus can do what he pleases." At best, revolt is in the mind, and brief.

Prometheus did believe he might free himself. But in the end, he realizes he was never free. It is Zeus who is free and he who is the slave, wiped out by the on-coming storm. "There in the squirls of lightning I see Zeus. His hands are not tied. I am burning in my own fire."

That seems to be Lowell's final judgment on Prometheus, for there is an air of finality about the whole play. What seems at first merely the idea of the minor servants of Zeus—that Zeus controls, and Prometheus is unable to break loose from that yoke—becomes, towards the end, the sense of the play. "Soon you will learn that standing up to Zeus is giving in to Zeus. You will stand because your chains force you to stand. But Zeus stands because he wants to stand and is unable to change."

Certainly, set against the background of Lowell's ideas of history, Prometheus must be seen as a victim rather than the leader of a successful revolt. History, for Lowell, is an endless series of tyrannies, each bad, each overthrown and restored and destroyed again; the past is no better or worse than the present; there is no such thing as progress. At best, we may have a gradual wearing away into nothingness. "You are timid about speaking out against Zeus, yet you seem to chirp and sigh for good old days. They were never good. We come from a snake wrapped in a mud-egg. We have struggled to where we are by living through a succession of tyrannies."

A moment of progress in a sea of entropy means nothing. A revolutionary can climb only so many steps before the stairway gives way and falls into ruin. "I could settle for a succession of gods, each a little stronger, and more intelligent than the last. Small loss to us, and some solace . . . All's shining, all stays in motion, the pace keeps rising. Why rising, though? Suppose the pace were to slow. Things, things! There's the unreason. No one has ever seen bottom through that life-giving blank. No one will step across the last line of space, or walk back through the atoms and microbes to time's beginning. No one will climb the end-step. Think of life cooling. No, I think of fire. Fire will be the first absolute power, and the last to rule."

Fire to Lowell is a symbol of what lies at the back of the universe, its substance, the raw energy, if we were to use the terms of physics, or the essence, if we were to use Plato's. Fire is not just that burning entropy that turns each of us into ashes, and even the gods. It is also, in this play, the imagination of man and the gift that Prometheus gave to man, his sense of discrimination, his ability to think, his gift of words. This much we find in Lowell's poems, when he is talking of fire. But there is more. For Prometheus finds 'a mind in things,' and that supernatural intelligence is also a kind of fire, burning through each rock like a forest fire moving over a mountain range. The fire of electrons, and the fire of the mind, both are the fires of destruction. "Once I hoped my fire would subdue the fire of destruction, but perhaps the two fires are the same. Fire is the beginning. . . . Yes, because of us, the fire is already rising to bury the gods. I will be buried in fire. No one will brush the burning ashes from our backs."

Politically, Lowell seems equally pessimistic about the chances of a revolution. Cronus, the old god, has aspects of Eisenhower, Chamberlain or Macmillan about him; when Zeus and Prometheus overthrow him, they feel like the new frontiersmen sweeping into Washington. But then Kennedy gave way to Johnson and what had seemed like an exciting overthrow of the old congealed and became hard, almost a worse tyranny since it was so much more athletic and intrusive. Neither history as a whole, nor politics in the short term, seems very promising to Lowell; both inevitably degenerate. As a kind of mastermind for Zeus's coup, Prometheus must now suffer the fate of all who get too close to the powerful and remind them of their ignorance; striking out on his own gets him nowhere. He is imprisoned and scorned.

Prometheus, then, is hamstrung. Continually imagining, aspiring, inventing, searching; forever falling away, unsuccessful, somehow baffled. For a politician, whether human or divine, this must be fatal.

But for a poet, what better situation to find oneself in! Prometheus is, as we have seen, in many ways a part of Lowell (after all, in writing a play of this length, some of his own picture of himself must have crept in), and if for a moment we imagine that Prometheus's situation is one that Lowell has experienced, at times, then think how it must enlarge one.

One must fight for some kind of truth, even when knowing it is never actually attainable. One must acknowledge that neither god nor the president has any real power over one, even though one goes on obeying both; one must continually rebel, and never reach freedom. As the chorus says of Prometheus, "We could never bear your punishment, or live with the thoughts that clash through your clear mind."

Because he has borne this suffering and because he has managed to show us just a few of the thoughts buffeting his mind, Lowell has managed to make a play that will last. It lasts because he has set up the conflicts within our own minds. And he has not resolved them, even in the end.

Prometheus is left waiting for Zeus's storm cloud and hawk to slam into him, smashing at him, devouring his bowels. Yet it is not clear whether Zeus will destroy him or not. It is not even certain that Prometheus will not save Zeus and stave off the inevitable decay of the regime. Lowell is guarding his mystery.

For the play would be less if it were more definite in making an end. He could have made a flatly programmatic drama out of the Prometheus story. But Lowell knows that the purpose of a work of art is not to make statements solely, but to keep those statements alive in the minds of its audience long after the performance. A play that tells us one thing may be registered and forgotten like a lecture. But one that raises questions makes us worry over it, trying to work out our own answers. Continually to be thought about—what else is fame? Or longevity, for a work of art? Instead of driving toward some point, Lowell only appears to drive toward some point—while actually enmeshing us in his own battles. We are drawn one way and then another. We are torn back and forth, and in the end we want to discover what is going on, what Lowell really thinks. For this we may have to turn back to the poems or the play itself, re-reading, studying, moving toward our own saddened, or enflamed, truth.

From *Works,* 1 (Autumn 1967), 120-26.

LOUIS MARTZ

Notebook

ROBERT LOWELL'S *Notebook 1967-68* shows a remarkable emergence from the pit of bitterness and despair that marked his volumes of only a few years ago, *For the Union Dead* and *Near the Ocean*. In those books one felt a misery and weariness of life represented in lines such as

> Only man thinning out his kind
> sounds through the Sabbath noon, the blind
> swipe of the pruner and his knife
> busy about the tree of life . . .

Lowell has not at all lost his awareness of the ugliness present in our world, as it cracks and reforms. He is intimately involved with the political issues of the day and he never forgets the brutalities of the past, whether they be the work of a Hitler or an Attila. But the poems in this *Notebook* are irradiated with the flow of love, an abundance of affection that begins with the happiness of having a ten-year-old daughter and a lasting marriage, and then floods out from the many intimate poems of domestic life to touch and enfold friends and relatives, ancient and modern, personal and poetical. Thus the affections of the book move out to embrace father, grandfather, aunts, schoolmates, along with Allen Tate, John Berryman, Peter Taylor, Randall Jarrell, Ted Roethke, Pound, Eliot, Williams, Frost, and many, many others, including Harpo Marx. What we are watching here is the flow of a poet's mind and thoughts, working upon the moments, lives, events, and intuitions that have struck his imagination. Sometimes the impulse lies in a painting:

> Manet's bourgeois husband takes the tiller at Cannes,
> the sea is right, the virgin's cocky boater,
> naive as the moon, streams with its heartstring ribbons—

Or perhaps it is a memory of King David in old age:

> Two or three times a night, and for a month,
> we wrang the night-sweat from his shirt and sheets;
> on the fortieth day, we brought him Abishag,
> and he recovered, and he knew her not—

Or it may be some historical figure, Sir Thomas More, Cato the Younger, Alexander.

Wherever the scene, whether in Cambridge, Mexico, Caracas, Maine, or New York City, one feels the spur of this affection quickening the poet's vision and stirring his wit to passages of a brilliance and ironic humor that excel some of the finest parts of his earlier poetry. Consider, for example, the wry, self-conscious humor of Lowell's treatment of his part in the march on the Pentagon:

> Where two or three were heaped together, or fifty,
> mostly white-haired, or bald, or women . . . sadly
> unfit to follow their dream, I sat in sunset
> shade of their Bastille, the Pentagon,
> nursing leg and arch-cramps, my cowardly,
> foolhardy heart; and heard, alas, more speeches,
> though the words took heart now to show how weak
> we were, and right. An MP sergeant kept
> repeating, "March slowly through them. Don't even brush
> anyone sitting down." They tiptoed through us
> in single file, and then their second wave
> trampled us flat and back. Health to those who held,
> health to the green steel head . . . to the kind hands
> that helped me stagger to my feet, and flee.

This is the kind of awareness that runs throughout the poetry, an awareness of the ridiculous figure that one may cut at the age of fifty (the age that Lowell celebrates gingerly throughout this volume), along with a dogged sense of the rightness and perhaps the ultimate justification of those who thus so weakly seek the right, as they see it. One finds here a similar poem on the trial of Dr. Spock and a remarkable poem to Eugene McCarthy, perhaps as fine a poem as ever was addressed to a politician who could not quite make it all the way:

> I love you so. . . . Gone? Who will swear you wouldn't
> have done good to the country, that fulfillment wouldn't
> have done good to you—the father, as Freud says:
> you? We've so little faith that anyone
> ever makes anything better . . .
> 　　　　　　　　　　Picking a quarrel
> with you is like picking the petals of the daisies—
> the game, the passing crowds, the rapid young
> still brand your hand with sunflecks . . . coldly willing
> to smash the ball past those who bought the park.

It seems a good characterization, but perhaps the most significant words are the first four: "I love you so," coming strangely, addressed to a Senator, and yet giving a fair summation of the mood that makes this Lowell's best volume since *Life Studies*.

In many ways, this is perhaps Lowell's richest, as it certainly is his longest
volume of poetry, consisting of almost three hundred sonnets! Yes, sonnets,
or so they seem to me in spite of Lowell's statement in his "Afterthought" that
"the poems in this book are written as one poem, jagged in pattern, but not
a conglomeration or sequence of related material." Clearly Lowell wishes us
to regard the book as a unity of some kind, written in what he calls "fourteen
line unrhymed blank verse sections." Then he goes on to say, "I fear I have
failed to avoid the themes and gigantism of the sonnet." I suppose that
"gigantism" implies the hubris of many traditional sonnets, straining for
greatness and autonomy within their narrow cells. Yet these poems have the
integrity of the traditional sonnet. They begin with sharp openings, thematic
lines such as: "Those awful figures of Yankee prehistory"; "Like Henry VIII,
Mohammed got religion"; "No folly can secularize the sacred cow"; "The
green paint's always peeling from the prospect"; "The old king enters his study
with the police"; "The book is finished and the air is lighter." With such
strong openings each poem tends toward a strict separation from its preceding
poem, while each "section" often develops in a way reminiscent of the old
petrarchan mode, with a break and a turning toward a resolution somewhere
around the eighth or ninth line. Thus in the second "section" of the book we
see how the "octave" of the poem (actually nine lines) sets up the ironic figure
of the helpless fly, like an airplane useless in its strength; and then in the last
five lines we see the abrupt shift to a painful realization of death, pitiful even
in the fly, more pitiful in its sense of the futility of the mighty fallen:

> A repeating fly, blueblack, thumbthick—so gross,
> it seems apocalyptic in our house—
> whams back and forth across the nursery bed
> manned by a madhouse of stuffed animals,
> not one a fighter. It is like a plane
> gunning potato bugs or Arabs on the screen—
> one of the mighty . . . one of the helpless. It
> bumbles and bumps its brow on this and that,
> making a short, unhealthy life the shorter.
> I kill it, and another instant's added
> to the horrifying mortmain of
> ephemera: keys, drift, sea-urchin shells,
> packratted off with joy, the dead fly swept
> under the carpet, wrinkling to fulfillment.

This movement is characteristic of perhaps a quarter of the poems in this
volume, while the use of imagery in this poem is also characteristic, involving
hints of war, while at the same time being fully aware of the domestic scene
in which the poet lives. In other poems here Lowell uses either the whiplash-
ending characteristic of Sidney's sonnets or the muted couplet by which Shakespeare binds his sonnets into an understated unity. One can see the last kind

of movement with particular strength in a sonnet entitled "Across the Yard:
La Ignota"—a poem dedicated to a faded prima donna:

> The soprano's bosoms point to the joy of God,
> Brunhild who would not rule her voice for God—
> she has to sing to fill such windows, hang
> such drapes: one is pink dust flipped back to scarlet,
> the other besmirched gauze—behind the first,
> a blown electric heater; behind the second,
> and placed as furniture, her footlocker
> with Munich stickers. No one really hires her;
> her grandiose, arched wooden window frames
> haven't felt paint or putty these twenty years;
> grass, dead since Kennedy, chokes the window box.
> Like a grackle, she flings her high aria through the trash. . . .
> When I was lost and green, I would have given
> the janitor three months' rent for this address.

The poet is present here from beginning to end. He sees her windows presumably from the window of his own apartment. It is his consciousness that fills
in the poignant timing, "dead since Kennedy," and it is the poet's memory of
his youthful enthusiasm that gives the sonnet-like twist in the last two lines.

Despite these sonnet-like effects, Lowell is right to feel that in some ways
the volume is to be read as a whole poem, since the controlling consciousness
of the poet is omnipresent, being frequently dramatized in addresses to his
friends, or mentioned in a letter opening "Dear Lowell," or embalmed in a
doctor's prescription. There are dozens of sonnets that we are bound to associate
with Lowell's childhood, education, and homes in Massachusetts, or in Maine.
The whole book stems from the reflective poise of this observer, standing at
the age of fifty, looking backward with appreciation of his life, even of its pains,
apprehending its relation to the world about him, whether that world include
the death of a poet's son or the occupation of the President's office at Columbia.
It will include Andrew Jackson, who, says Lowell, "despite appearances, stands
for the gunnery that widened suffrage"; while the poet's sympathy can also go
out to one who was a hero to the other side, as in the touching sonnet on the
suicide of a Japanese admiral:

> There's always enough sunrise in hell to gasp the breeze;
> the flower of what was left grew sweeter for them,
> two done people conversing with bamboo fans
> as if brushing the firefall from their yard—
> Admiral Onishi is still a cult to his juniors
> for launching the Kamikazes; he became an osprey
> by mistaking our armadas for game;
> his pilots loved him to annihilation.
> He chats in his garden, the sky is zigzags of fire.

One butchery is left; his wife keeps nagging.
Man and wife taste cup after cup of Scotch;
how garrulously they talk about their grandchildren,
and when the knife goes home, it goes home wrong. . . .
For eighteen hours you died with your hand in hers.

That sonnet alone should be enough to indicate the range and power of these poems, which are made both for browsing and for steady sequential reading. The wit, the love, the courage, the skill, the power of this poet's grasp on the world that we now own, all these qualities create a volume rich in wisdom, humor, and human dignity.

From *The Yale Review,* 59 (1969), 252-56.

WILLIAM MEREDITH

Looking Back

COMPLEX AND imperfect, like most of the accomplishments of serious men and women today, Robert Lowell's "Notebook 1967-68" is nevertheless a beautiful and major work. In what seems a propitiatory act to the modern god of chaos, the poet offers an account of his personal history as it has painstakingly ordered itself in images. It is the response of a racked but magnanimous mind, the response of a poet.

Lowell's work originally commanded attention because, among other virtues, it ranged over more human experience more generously than is common in modern poetry. Often the poet identified himself with people who had made historical errors, or with an artist who watched and understood such errors. His first major poem, "The Quaker Graveyard in Nantucket," goes beyond the conventional purposes of a wartime elegy for a dead sailor, to reckon up man's religious failures. Some years later when he made a secular reckoning in the title poem of "For the Union Dead" (1964), it was with the same sense of his own involvement.

In "Life Studies" (1959), the accounts of his family and of himself rise above the usual confessional poem in two respects. They are social criticism of the America they take place in, and they make serious moral judgments in which all the characters, including the speaker, share. Lowell's translations, which include dramatic versions of Racine, Aeschylus, Hawthorne and Melville, and the wide range of lyrics in "Imitations" (1961), sometimes distort their originals in order to give the new works an imaginative impact intended for an earlier time. The "Notebook" extends in surprising but not illogical ways some of these thrusts from earlier work.

Many of the events in the "Notebook" are drawn from our common history of recent months, our wars and demonstrations, our assassinations and riots. Others are intensely, even hermetically, private. But throughout burns a passionate intelligence, a conscience, which the reader feels is trustworthy. After the worst has been said, it can still mete out praise, it is accountable for blame. "In truth I seem to have felt mostly the joys of living; in remembering, in recording, thanks to the gift of the Muse, it is the pain," Lowell says at the end of the book.

It is a big book, two and a half times the length of "Lord Weary's Castle," the book that won Lowell a Pulitzer Prize in 1947, and we are asked to regard it as a single poem, though it is divided into self-contained stanzas with individual titles. "My meter, fourteen line unrhymed blank verse, is fairly strict

at first and elsewhere, but often corrupts in single lines to the freedom of prose.
Even with this license, I fear I have failed to avoid the themes and gigantism
of the sonnet."

If he does largely avoid those weary assets of the sonnet, it is because his
stanzas create their own decorum, a sequence of freely expanding images:

STALIN

Winds on the stems make them creak like things made by man;
a hedge of vines and bushes—three or four
kinds, grape leaf, elephant ear and alder,
an arabesque, imperfect and alive,
a hundred hues of green, the darkest shades
short of black, the palest leaf-backs far from white.
The state, if we could see behind the walls,
is woven of perishable vegetation.
Stalin? What shot him clawing up the tree of power—
millions plowed under like the crops they grew,
his intimates dying like the spider-bridegroom?
The large stomach could only chew success. What raised him
was the usual lust to break the icon,
joke cruelly, seriously, and be himself.

The movement here is from six lines of observed, wind-blown foliage,
through two lines where that foliage becomes a rational metaphor for the state,
into six final lines, where, with no pretext of rational transition, we are given
the anthropoid figure of Stalin ravaging an allegorical landscape. This is a usual
movement in the "Notebook" (not new to Lowell's work, but more systematic
here than before)— a shuttling between the reporter's view and the mystic's,
at an erratic pace designed to surprise us into binocular vision. "I lean heavily
to the rational, but am devoted to surrealism," he tells us in a prose "Afterthought."

His form is flexible, but it has the strength to contain not only this freedom
of image but the free association of events which constitutes his plot. A
notebook's continuity is simply the fabric of the writer's attentions and concerns. Its chronology is as quick as thought and as confusing as history. "My
plot rolls with the seasons," Lowell says. "The separate poems and sections are
opportunist and inspired by impulse." In these conditions, the unit of articula-
tion, the stanza-poem, creates a steady, rational reference.

As if to underscore this structure, many sections are pulled together by a
line or two of commanding energy—dramatic, rhetorical, metaphoric. These
conclusions are commonly the reverse of the quiet dying-away of a Shakespeare-
an couplet. They are an intense cutting-off, often too dense syntactically to
survive quotation. But here are several excerptable ones that bring the long
poem to moments of temporary repose. I point to these lines not as samples
of Lowell's lyric virtuosity—the book is shot through with that—but to make
the point that in the torrent of events and images, these resolutions occur

regularly. The stanzas are the stabilizing element, and lines like these delineate
the stanzas:

> The king is laughing, all his men are killed,
> he is shaken by the news, as well he might be.

> In the days of the freeze, we see a minor sun,
> our winter moon bled for the solar rose.

> fame, a bouquet in the niche of forgetfulness!

> Cattle have guts, but after the barn is burned,
> they will look at the sunset and tremble.

> in you, God knows, I've had the earthly life—
> we were kind of religious, we thought in images.

As the final quotation suggests, the poet's personal life is an important part
of the fabric. The poems to his wife and daughter include some of the most
sensitive and the most wide-ranging philosophically. A self-characterization, of
course, is the book's chief unity. It is a character more austere, less charming
than the dreamer in Berryman's "Dream Songs," perhaps the only recent work
to which the "Notebook" can be compared.

In filling out the character, Lowell has reworked a number of poems from
his earlier books, "Lord Weary's Castle," "The Mills of the Kavanaughs," "For
the Union Dead"—formative experiences to which the journal-keeper seems
to return naturally, as he reverts in new poems to events and persons we have
already met. People from books and history and the arts appear and talk to us.
Lowell is an intellectual man rather than an intellectual mind. History, literature and art are among the things that have vividly befallen him in an 18-month
period.

I suppose it is extravagant to speak of a book of poems as an act of
propitiation. But when one of our best poets—only Pound, Auden and Berryman can be named in the company now, I think—writes down all the patterns
of his mind, he seems to be saying they are fragments of order. The poet—in
all modesty, in all vanity— creates order, if at all, by arrangement. Where
human response is as accurate as this, it becomes a hopeful kind of human
sacrifice:

READING MYSELF

> Like millions, I took just pride and more than just,
> first striking matches that brought my blood to boiling;
> I memorized tricks to set the river on fire,
> somehow never wrote something to go back to.
> Even suppose I had finished with wax flowers
> and earned a pass to the minor slopes of Parnassus . . .

No honeycomb is built without a bee
adding circle to circle, cell to cell,
the wax and honey of a mausoleum—
this round dome proves its maker is alive,
the corpse of such insect lives preserved in honey,
prays that the perishable work live long
enough for the sweet-tooth bear to desecrate—
this open book . . . my open coffin.

From *The New York Times Book Review,* 15 June 1969, pp. 1, 27.

SELECTED BIBLIOGRAPHY

The two basic works are Hugh B. Staples' *Robert Lowell: The First Twenty Years* (New York: Farrar, Straus and Cudahy, 1962), and Jerome Mazzaro's *The Poetic Themes of Robert Lowell* (Ann Arbor: University of Michigan Press, 1965). Another important source is the November 1961 issue of the *Harvard Advocate*.

Alvarez, A. "A Talk with Robert Lowell." *Encounter*, 24 (Feb. 1965), 39-43. A careful interview.

Berman, David. "Robert Lowell and the Aristocratic Tradition." *Harvard Advocate*, 145 (Nov. 1961), 15-19. Personal, public, and literary tradition, and Lowell's treatment of them.

Blackmur, R.P. "Notes on Eleven Poets." *Kenyon Review*, 7 (1945), 339-52. Praises *Land of Unlikeness*, but worries about the "fractious vindictiveness" which he finds in the verse.

Bly, Robert. "Robert Lowell's *For the Union Dead.*" *Sixties*, 8 (1966), 93-96. Bly's own standards playing off Lowell's poems.

Braybrooke, Neville. "Robert Lowell and the Unjust Steward." *Dalhousie Review*, 44 (1964), 28-34. A study of the earlier work from the point of view of the parable of the unjust steward.

Cambon, Glauco. *"Dea Roma."* *Accent*, 20 (1960), 51-61. A good analysis of the significance of the figure of the city of Rome in Lowell's works.

Carne-Ross, D.S. "Conversation with Robert Lowell." *Delos*, 1 (1968), 165-75. Discussion of translation as tradition and influence in Lowell's work.

Carruth, Hayden. "Toward, Not Away From. . . . " *Poetry*, 101 (April 1962), 43-47. An intelligent enthusiasm for *Imitations*, as poetry, let aside translations.

Davison, Peter. "The Difficulty of Being Major." *Atlantic*, Oct. 1967, pp. 116-21. A consideration of Lowell's stature.

Fein, Richard. "Mary and Bellona: The War Poetry of Robert Lowell." *The Southern Review*, NS 1 (1965), 820-34. Conflict as metaphor and subject, in Lowell's earlier work.

Fremantle, Anne. *"Lord Weary's Castle,"* *Commonweal*, 27 December 1946, pp. 283-84. Excellent description of Lowell's characteristic poetic disciplines.

Goldman, Eric. "White House and the Intellectuals." *Harper's*, March 1969, pp. 4-7. On Lowell's refusal to attend the White House Festival of the Arts in June 1965.

Gray-Lews, Stephen W. "Too Late for Eden." *Cithara*, 5 (1966), 41-51. Dualism in *The Mills of the Kavanaughs*.

Gregory, Horace. "A Life Study as an Illumination of Life Conflicts." *Commonweal*, 3 July 1959, p. 356. An approach to *Life Studies*.

Gunn, Thom. "Excellences and Variety." *Yale Review*, 49 (1960), 295-305. Good statement of complaints about *Life Studies*.

Gunn, Thom. "Imitations and Originals." *Yale Review*, 51 (1962), 480-89. Good statement of complaints about *Imitations*.

Howard, Richard. "Voice of a Survivor." *The Nation,* 26 October 1964, pp. 278-80. A discussion of what he calls Lowell's "dialectic of revolution and reaction, of raid and retreat," particularly in *For the Union Dead.*

London, Michael, and Boyers, Robert, eds. *Robert Lowell: A Portrait of the Artist in his Time.* New York: David Lewis Publishers, 1970. Includes Frederick Seidel's *Paris Review* interview and an excellent checklist of Lowell material by Jerome Mazzaro, 1939-1968.

Martz, W. *The Achievement of Robert Lowell.* Glenview, Ill.: n.p., 1966. A general introduction, with selected poems.

Mills, Ralph J. "Robert Lowell." *Contemporary American Poetry.* New York: 1965. A solid study of the work through 1964.

Moon, Sam. "Master as Servant." *Poetry,* 108 (June 1966), 189-90. Analysis of *The Old Glory* as poetry.

Newlove, Donald. "Dinner at the Lowells'." *Esquire,* 72 (September 1969), 128-29. An erratic conversation.

Nims, John Frederick. "Two Catholic Poets." *Poetry,* 65 (1944-45), 264-68. Considers Lowell in his early work as a Catholic.

Parkinson, Thomas, ed. *Robert Lowell, A Collection of Critical Essays.* Englewood Cliffs, N. J.: Prentice Hall, 1968. An anthology arguing that Lowell "as much as any current poet deserves systematic study in universities."

Price, Jonathan R. "The Making of Prometheus Bound." *Yale Alumni Magazine,* June 1967, pp. 30-37. A study of the interaction of director and playwright, in rehearsals, and an interpretation of the play.

Ransom, John Crowe. "A Look Backwards and a Note of Hope." *Harvard Advocate,* 145 (November 1961), 22-23. Ransom's own view of the risks and the conquests in the course of Lowell's career.

Rizzardi, Alfredo. *La Condizione Americana, Studi Su Poeti Nord-americani.* Bologna: n.p., 1960. A very European view: by a man who knows Lowell well.

Salmagundi, Vol. 1, No. 4. (1966-67). A special issue on Robert Lowell.

"Second Chance." *Time,* 2 June 1967, pp. 67-74. Cover story on Lowell.

Spacks, Patricia. "From Satire to Description." *Yale Review,* 58 (1968), 232-48. Compares Lowell's translations of Juvenal with Samuel Johnson's.

Spivack, K. "Lowell." *Poetry,* 112 (June 1970), 191-93. Consideration of Lowell's most recent work.

Wain, John. *"For the Union Dead."* *New Republic,* 17 October 1964, pp. 21-23. Good description of Lowell's reputation at the time, and a consequent dissection of the poems in this volume.

Wiebe, Dallas E. "Mr. Lowell and Mr. Edwards." *Wisconsin Studies in Contemporary Literature,* 3 (1962), 21-31. A close study of the Jonathan Edwards poems.

Williamson, A. "Lowell." *Poetry,* 112 (January 1970), 281-82. A discussion of the most recent work.